POPE
BENEDICT XVI
IN THE
HOLY LAND

Studies in
Judaism and Christianity

Exploration of Issues in the Contemporary Dialogue Between Christians and Jews

Editors
Lawrence Boadt, CSP
Kevin A. Lynch, CSP
Yehezkel Landau
Dr. Peter Petit
Dr. Elena Procario-Foley
Dr. Ann Riggs
Michael Kerrigan, CSP

 A STIMULUS BOOK

POPE BENEDICT XVI IN THE HOLY LAND

*with Christian and Jewish Perspectives
by Michael McGarry, CSP, and
Deborah Weissman*

Pope Benedict XVI

A STIMULUS BOOK

PAULIST PRESS ◆ NEW YORK ◆ MAHWAH, NJ

Cover design by Sharyn Banks
Book design by Lynn Else

Cover photo © Reuters/Pool News

Library of Congress Cataloging-in-Publication Data

Benedict XVI, Pope, 1927–
   Pope Benedict XVI in the Holy Land : with Christian and Jewish perspectives / Pope Benedict XVI.
      p. cm.
   Addresses delivered May 8–15, 2009.
   "A Stimulus book."
   ISBN 978-0-8091-4672-7 (alk. paper)
   1. Benedict XVI, Pope, 1927—Travel—Palestine. 2. Palestine—Description and travel. 3. Papal visits—Palestine. 4. Palestine in Christianity. 5. Catholic Church—Relations—Judaism. 6. Judaism—Relations—Catholic Church. I. Title.
   BX1378.6.B4545 2011
   252′.02—dc22
                                                            2010027918

Published by Paulist Press
997 Macarthur Boulevard
Mahwah, New Jersey 07430

www.paulistpress.com

Printed and bound in the
United States of America

CONTENTS

CONTENTS

Contents

CONTENTS

DAY EIGHT: MAY 15, 2009

CHRISTIAN AND JEWISH PERSPECTIVES ON THE HOLY FATHER'S VISIT

INTRODUCTION

Michael Kerrigan, CSP

Comparisons are repeatedly made between the pontificate of Pope Benedict XVI and his predecessor Pope John Paul II. This is inevitable given the prominence of Pope John Paul II, whose travels included 104 apostolic visits over twenty-six years during his pontificate. Papal visits draw media attention as the religious leader of the Catholic Church journeys to visit, to meet, and to speak with the people in the local area. The pope's words are carefully evaluated and his actions closely observed.

Pope Benedict XVI's decision to accept President Shimon Peres's invitation to visit Israel and to come to the Holy Land as a personal pilgrim would become another occasion for papal comparison that would be closely scrutinized. The pope's visit would be evaluated against his predecessor's visit in 2000. The human dimension of making comparisons with others invariably arises. Both popes shared the common experience of personally witnessing the Nazi terror of World War II: John Paul II in Poland and Benedict XVI in Germany in his forced participation in the Nazi youth corps.

Prior to his election as pope on April 19, 2005, Cardinal Joseph Ratzinger visited the Holy Land as a theologian who lectured and as one who prayed in retreat while visiting Jerusalem's holy sites. The May 2009 visit would be different, especially given some of the controversial events involving his papacy that occurred in the months leading up to it.

This book chronicles the 2009 papal visit to the Holy Land by following the itinerary and providing the words spoken at the various locations. These are the pope's own words as a pilgrim on a journey of faith and as the leader of the Catholic Church. As another volume in the STIMULUS BOOKS to promote and foster mutual understanding between Jews and Christians, this collection of the pope's words is complemented by concluding reflections from two prominent scholars and participants in the Jewish-Christian dialogue at the Tantur Ecumenical Institute: Rev. Michael McGarry, CSP, and Dr. Deborah Weissman, both of whom witnessed firsthand the local responses to the papal visit.

Since the words and actions of Pope Benedict XVI's visit are going to be viewed through the prism of what Pope John Paul II said and did in 2000, especially at Yad Vashem, the Western Wall, visits with political leaders and elected officials, it may be helpful for purposes of comparison to read this book along with *John Paul II in the Holy Land: In His Own Words* (Paulist Press, 2005) as a way to appreciate the significance of this papal pilgrimage.

As you read through this book and view the photos from this historic papal visit, as well as ponder the profound insights and thoughtful perspectives of Fr. McGarry and Dr. Weissman, use this opportunity to reflect upon the mystery of God's plans for humanity revealed among peoples of religious faiths to continue to learn, to listen, to dialogue, and to seek ways to trust one another.

May we continue to pray for peace, ongoing interreligious dialogue, and better mutual understanding among the peoples of the three great world religions living in the Holy Land—Judaism, Christianity, and Islam.

Michael Kerrigan, CSP
Editor, Paulist Press

ITINERARY

Pope Benedict XVI's Pilgrimage to the Holy Land

DAY ONE

May 8, 2009

1. Arrives in Amman, Jordan
2. Welcoming ceremony at the Queen Alia International Airport in Amman
3. Visit to Regina Pacis Centre in Amman
4. Courtesy visit to their majesties, the king and queen of Jordan, at the royal palace in Amman-Husseiny

DAY TWO

May 9, 2009

1. Private Mass in the chapel of the apostolic nunciature of Amman
2. Visit to the ancient basilica of the Memorial of Moses on Mount Nebo
3. Blessing of the cornerstone of Madaba University of the Latin Patriarchate
4. Visit to the Hashemite museum and the Al-Hussein Bin Talal Mosque in Amman

5. Meeting with Muslim religious leaders, members of the diplomatic corps, and rectors of universities in Jordan, in front of the mosque al-Hussein bin Talal in Amman
6. Celebration of Vespers with priests, men and women religious, seminarians, and ecclesial movements in the Greek-Melkite Cathedral of Saint-Georges in Amman

DAY THREE
May 10, 2009

1. Mass celebrated at the Amman International Stadium
2. Recitation of the *Regina Coeli* at the Amman International Stadium
3. Luncheon with patriarchs, bishops, and papal entourage at the Latin Vicariate of Amman
4. Visit to the site of the baptism of Christ, at Bethany Beyond the Jordan
5. Blessing of the foundation stones of the Latin and Greek Melkite churches at Bethany Beyond the Jordan

DAY FOUR
May 11, 2009

1. Private Mass in the chapel of the apostolic nunciature in Amman
2. Farewell ceremony at the Queen Alia International Airport in Amman

3. Departure from the Queen Alia International
   Airport of Amman (Jordan) for Ben Gurion
   International Airport of Tel Aviv (Israel)
4. Welcoming ceremony at Ben Gurion International
   Airport of Tel Aviv
5. Courtesy visit to the president of the State of Israel
   at the presidential palace in Jerusalem
6. Visit to the Yad Vashem Memorial in Jerusalem
7. Meeting with organizations involved in
   interreligious dialogue at the auditorium of
   Notre Dame Center in Jerusalem

DAY FIVE
May 12, 2009

1. Visit to the Dome of the Rock on Temple Mount
   in Jerusalem
2. Courtesy visit to the Grand Mufti of Jerusalem at
   the Mount of the Temple
3. Visit to the Western Wall in Jerusalem
4. Courtesy visit to the two chief rabbis of Israel at
   the Hechal Shlomo Centre of Jerusalem
5. *Regina Coeli* prayer with the ordinaries of the Holy
   Land in the Upper Room in Jerusalem
6. Short visit to the Co-cathedral of the Latins in
   Jerusalem
7. Luncheon with the ordinaries of the Holy Land, the
   abbots, and the papal entourage in the Patriarchate
   of the Latins in Jerusalem
8. Mass in the Valley of Josaphat in Jerusalem

DAY SIX
May 13, 2009

1. Welcoming ceremony in the square in front of the presidential palace in Bethlehem
2. Mass in Manger Square, Bethlehem
3. Luncheon with the ordinaries of the Holy Land, the Franciscan community, and the papal entourage at the Casa Nova Monastery in Bethlehem
4. Private visit to the Grotto of the Nativity in Bethlehem
5. Visit to the Caritas Baby Hospital in Bethlehem
6. Visit to the Aida Refugee Camp in Bethlehem
7. Courtesy visit to the president of the Palestine National Authority in the presidential palace of Bethlehem
8. Farewell ceremony in the courtyard of the presidential palace

DAY SEVEN
May 14, 2009

1. Mass on the Mount of Precipice in Nazareth
2. Luncheon with the ordinaries of the Holy Land, the Franciscan community, and the papal entourage in the Franciscan convent of Nazareth
3. Meeting with the Israeli prime minister in the Franciscan convent of Nazareth
4. Greetings to religious leaders of Galilee in the auditorium of the Shrine of the Annunciation in Nazareth

5. Visit to the Grotto of the Nativity in Nazareth
6. Celebration of Vespers with bishops, priests, men and women religious, and ecclesial and pastoral movements of Galilee in the Upper Basilica of the Annunciation in Nazareth

DAY EIGHT

May 15, 2009

1. Private Mass in the chapel of the apostolic delegation to Jerusalem
2. Ecumenical meeting in the throne hall of the Greek Orthodox Patriarchate of Jerusalem
3. Visit to the Holy Sepulchre in Jerusalem
4. Visit to the Armenian patriarchal church of St. James in Jerusalem
5. Departure ceremony at Ben Gurion International Airport in Tel Aviv
6. Departure by plane from the Ben Gurion International Airport in Tel Aviv (Israel) for Ciampino Airport (Rome)

Day One

May 8, 2009

1

INTERVIEW OF THE HOLY FATHER DURING THE FLIGHT TO THE HOLY LAND

Father Lombardi: *Your Holiness, thank you very much for giving us the opportunity once again for a meeting with you at the beginning of such an important and demanding journey. Among other things, it allows us to wish you a good journey and to assure you that we will play our part in spreading the messages that you wish to convey to us. As usual, the questions I am about to ask are the result of a collection of questions proposed by my colleagues here present. I shall put these questions to you myself, purely for ease of logistics, but they were in fact produced by a joint effort.*

Your Holiness, this journey is taking place at a very delicate moment for the Middle East: there are strong tensions— at the time of the crisis in Gaza, there was even speculation that you might decide not to come. At the same time, a few days after your journey, the principal political leaders of Israel and the Palestinian Authority will also be meeting President Obama. Do you think you can offer a contribution to the peace process that now seems to have become deadlocked?

The Holy Father: Good morning! First, I should like to thank all of you for the work that you do, and let us all wish one another a good journey, a good pilgrimage, a good return journey. As for the question, certainly I shall seek to contribute to peace not as an individual but in the name of the Catholic Church and of the Holy See. We are not a political power, but a spiritual force, and this spiritual force is a reality that can contribute to advances in the peace process. I see three levels.

First, as believers we are convinced that prayer is a real force: it opens the world to God. We are convinced that God listens and that he can act in history. I think that if millions of people—millions of believers—all pray, this is truly a force that influences and can contribute to moving forward the cause of peace. Second, we are seeking to assist in the formation of consciences. The conscience is the human capacity to perceive the truth, but this capacity is often impeded by particular interests. And to break free from these interests, to open up more to the truth, to true values, is a major undertaking: it is a task of the Church to help us to know true criteria, true values, and to free us from particular interests. And so, third, we also speak—no doubt about it—to reason: precisely because we are not a political force, we can perhaps more easily, and in the light of the faith, see the true criteria. We can assist in understanding what contributes to peace and we can appeal to reason, we can support positions that are truly reasonable. This we have already done, and we wish to do so again now and in the future.

Fr. Lombardi: *Thank you, Your Holiness. The second question: as a theologian, you have reflected particularly on the common roots shared by Christians and Jews. How is it that, despite the efforts toward dialogue, misunderstandings often occur? How do you see the future of dialogue between the two communities?*

The Holy Father: The important thing is that we really do have the same roots, the same books of the Old Testament, a book which—both for the Jews and for us—conveys Revelation. Yet of course, after two thousand years of distinct, not to say separate, histories, it is no wonder if misunderstandings arise, because very different traditions of interpretation, language, and thought have been formed. There is, so to speak, a very different "semantic cosmos," such that the same words used in the two traditions mean different things; and with this use of words that, in the course of history, have acquired different meanings, misunderstandings obviously arise. We must each do all we can to learn the language of the other, and it seems to me that we are making great progress here. Today it is possible for young people, future teachers of theology, to study in Jerusalem, at the Hebrew University, and Jews have academic contacts with us: thus an encounter is taking place between one "semantic cosmos" and the other. Let us learn from one another and let us go forward along the path of true dialogue. Let us each learn from the other, and I am sure and convinced that we will make progress. And this will also help peace; indeed it will help mutual love.

Father Lombardi: *Your Holiness, this journey has two essential dimensions of interreligious dialogue—with Islam and with Judaism. Are the two directions completely separate from one another, or will there also be a common message concerning the three Abrahamic religions?*

The Holy Father: Certainly there is also a common message and there will be opportunities to highlight it. Notwithstanding our diverse origins, we have common roots because, as I have already said, Christianity is born from the Old Testament, and the Scripture of the New Testament would not exist without the Old, because it makes constant reference to "the Scriptures," that is, to the Old Testament. Islam too was born in a world where both Judaism and the various branches of Christianity—Judeo-Christianity, Antiochene Christianity, and Byzantine Christianity—were all present, and all these circumstances are reflected in the Koranic tradition, with the result that we have much in common in terms of our origins and our faith in the one God. So it is important on the one hand to have bilateral dialogues—with the Jews and with Islam—and then also trilateral dialogue. I myself was the cofounder of a foundation for dialogue among the three religions, at which leading figures like Metropolitan Damaskinos and the Chief Rabbi of France René Samuel Sirat and others came together. This foundation also issued an edition of the books of the three religions: the Koran, the New Testament, and the Old Testament. So the trilateral dialogue must go forward: it is extremely important for peace and also—let us say—for living one's own religion well.

Father Lombardi: *One final question. Your Holiness: you have often spoken of the problem of the declining number of Christians in the Middle East and especially in the Holy Land. It is a phenomenon with various causes of a political, economic, and social character. What can be done in practice to assist the Christian presence in the region? What contribution do you hope to make with your journey? Is there hope for these Christians in the future? Do you have a particular message for the Christians in Gaza who will come to meet you in Bethlehem?*

The Holy Father: Certainly there is hope, because while this is a difficult moment, as you have mentioned, it is also a time of hope for a new beginning, for a new impetus along the path to peace. We wish above all to encourage the Christians in the Holy Land and throughout the Middle East to remain, to offer their contribution in their countries of origin: they are an important component of the life and culture of these regions. In practice, what the Church brings—in addition to words of encouragement and common prayer—are chiefly schools and hospitals. In this sense, we have thoroughly practical establishments here. Our schools educate a generation that will be able to make its presence felt in life today, in public life. The Catholic Church is opening a University in Jordan, which strikes me as an important setting in which young people—both Muslims and Christians—will meet, will learn together, and where a Christian intelligentsia can be formed that is suitably prepared to work for peace. But in general, our schools provide a very important opportunity that opens up a future for the Christians, and the hospitals make our presence visible. Moreover, there are many Christian associations that help Christians in different ways, and with practical assistance they encourage them to stay. So I hope that the Christians really will find the courage, the humility, and the patience to remain in these lands, and to offer their contribution to the future of these lands.

Father Lombardi: *Thank you, Your Holiness, with these replies you have helped us to put our journey in context from a spiritual point of view, and from a cultural point of view. Once more, I express to you my own good wishes, and those of all my colleagues on this flight, including the others who are flying to the Holy Land at this time, in order to take part and to assist, through their reporting, in attaining a positive outcome for this demanding mission of yours. May you and all your collaborators have a good journey, and to my colleagues I say: Buon lavoro!*

2

WELCOMING CEREMONY AT QUEEN ALIA INTERNATIONAL AIRPORT, AMMAN

Your Majesties,
Your Excellencies,
Dear Brother Bishops,
Dear Friends,

It is with joy that I greet all of you here present, as I begin my first visit to the Middle East since my election to the Apostolic See, and I am pleased to set foot upon the soil of the Hashemite Kingdom of Jordan, a land so rich in history, home to so many ancient civilizations, and so deeply imbued with religious significance for Jews, Christians, and Muslims. I thank His Majesty King Abdullah II for his kind words of welcome, and I offer my particular congratulations in this year that marks the tenth anniversary of his accession to the throne. In greeting His Majesty, I extend heartfelt good wishes to all members of the royal family and the government, and to all the people of the kingdom. I greet His Beatitude Fouad Twal and His Beatitude Theophilus III and also other patriarchs and bishops here present, especially those with pastoral responsibilities in Jordan. I look forward to celebrating the liturgy at Saint George's Cathedral tomorrow evening and at the International Stadium on Sunday together with you, dear bishops, and so many of the faithful entrusted to your care.

I come to Jordan as a pilgrim, to venerate holy places that have played such an important part in some of the key events of biblical history. At Mount Nebo, Moses led his people to within sight of the land that would become their home, and here he died and was laid to rest. At Bethany Beyond the Jordan, John the Baptist preached and bore witness to Jesus, whom he baptized in the waters of the river that gives this land its name. In the coming days, I shall visit both these holy places, and I shall have the joy of blessing the foundation stones of churches that are to be built at the traditional site of the Lord's baptism. The opportunity that Jordan's Catholic

Tony Gentile/REUTERS

Pope Benedict XVI is welcomed by Jordan's Queen Rania as he arrives at Queen Alia International Airport in Amman.

community enjoys to build public places of worship is a sign of this country's respect for religion, and on their behalf, I want to say how much this openness is appreciated. Religious freedom is, of course, a fundamental human right, and it is my fervent hope and prayer that respect for all the inalienable rights and the dignity of every man and woman will come to be increasingly affirmed and defended, not only throughout the Middle East, but in every part of the world.

My visit to Jordan gives me a welcome opportunity to speak of my deep respect for the Muslim community, and to pay tribute to the leadership shown by His Majesty the King in promoting a better understanding of the virtues proclaimed by Islam. Now that some years have passed since the publication of the Amman Message and the Amman Interfaith Message, we can say that these worthy initiatives have achieved much good in furthering an alliance of civilizations between the West and the Muslim world, confounding the predictions of those who consider violence and conflict inevitable. Indeed the Kingdom of Jordan has long been at the forefront of initiatives to promote peace in the Middle East and throughout the world, encouraging interreligious dialogue, supporting efforts to find a just solution to the Israeli-Palestinian conflict, welcoming refugees from neighboring Iraq, and seeking to curb extremism. I cannot let this opportunity pass without calling to mind the pioneering efforts for peace in the region made by the late King Hussein. How fitting that my meeting tomorrow with Muslim religious leaders, the diplomatic corps, and University rectors should take place in the mosque that bears his name. May his commitment to the resolution of the region's conflicts continue to bear fruit in efforts to promote lasting peace and true justice for all who live in the Middle East.

Dear friends, at the seminar held in Rome last autumn by the Catholic-Muslim Forum, the participants examined the central role played in our respective religious traditions by the commandment of love. I hope very much that this visit, and indeed all the initiatives designed to foster good relations between Christians and Muslims, will help us to grow in love for the Almighty and Merciful God, and in fraternal love for one another. Thank you for your welcome. Thank you for your attention. May God grant Your Majesties happiness and long life! May he bless Jordan with prosperity and peace!

3

VISIT TO THE REGINA PACIS CENTER

Your Beatitudes,
Your Excellencies,
Dear Friends,

I am very happy to be here with you this afternoon, and to greet each of you and your family members, wherever they may be. I thank His Beatitude Patriarch Fouad Twal for his kind words of welcome and in a special way I wish to acknowledge the presence among us of Bishop Selim Sayegh, whose vision and labors for this center, together with those of His Beatitude Patriarch Emeritus Michel Sabbah, are today honored through the blessing of the new extensions, which has just taken place. I also wish to greet with great affection the central committee members, the Comboni Sisters, and the dedicated lay staff, including those who work in the center's many community branches and units. Your reputation for outstanding professional competence, compassionate care, and resolute promotion of the rightful place in society of those with special needs is well known here and throughout the kingdom. To the young people present, I thank you for your moving welcome. It is a great joy for me to be with you.

As you know, my visit to the Our Lady of Peace Center here in Amman is the first stop along my journey of pilgrimage. Like countless pilgrims before me, it is now my turn to satisfy that profound wish to touch, to draw solace from, and to venerate the places where Jesus lived, the places which were made holy by his presence. Since apostolic times, Jerusalem has been the primary place of pilgrimage for Christians, but earlier still, in the ancient Near East, Semitic peoples built sacred shrines in order to mark and commemorate a divine presence or action. And ordinary people would travel to these centers carrying a portion of the fruits of their land and livestock to offer in homage and thanksgiving.

Dear friends, every one of us is a pilgrim. We are all drawn forward, with purpose, along God's path. Naturally, then, we tend to look back on life—sometimes with regrets or hurts, often with thanksgiving and appreciation—and we also look ahead—sometimes with trepidation or anxiety, but always with expectation and hope, knowing too that there are others who encourage us along the way. I know that the journeys that have led many of you to the Regina Pacis Center have been marked by suffering or trial. Some of you struggle courageously with disabilities, others of you have endured rejection, and some of you are drawn to this place of peace simply for encouragement and support. Of particular importance, I know, is the center's great success in promoting the rightful place of the disabled in society and in ensuring that suitable training and opportunities are provided to facilitate such integration. For this foresight and determination you all deserve great praise and encouragement!

At times, it is difficult to find a reason for what appears only as an obstacle to be overcome or even as pain—physical or emotional—to be endured. Yet faith and understanding help us to see a horizon beyond our own selves in order to imagine life as God does. God's unconditional love, which gives life to every human individual, points to a meaning and purpose for all human life. His is a saving love (cf. John 12:32). As Christians profess, it is through the Cross that Jesus in fact draws us into eternal life, and in so doing indicates to us the way ahead—the way of hope which guides every step we take along the way, so that we too become bearers of that hope and charity for others.

Friends, unlike the pilgrims of old, I do not come bearing gifts or offerings. I come simply with one intention, a hope: to pray for the precious gift of unity and peace, most specifically for the Middle East. Peace for individuals, for parents and children, for communities, peace for Jerusalem, for the Holy Land, for the region, peace for the entire human family; the lasting peace born of justice, integrity, and compassion, the peace that arises from humility, forgiveness, and the profound desire to live in harmony as one.

Prayer is hope in action. And in fact, true reason is contained in prayer: we come into loving contact with the one God, the universal Creator, and in so doing we come to realize the futility of human divisions and prejudices. We sense the wondrous possibilities that open up before us when our hearts are converted to God's truth, to his design for each of us and our world.

Dear young friends, to you in particular I wish to say that standing in your midst I draw strength from God. Your experience of trials, your witness to compassion, and your determination to overcome the obstacles you encounter, encourage me in the belief that suffering can bring about change for the good. In our own trials, and standing alongside others in their struggles, we glimpse the essence of our humanity; we become, as it were, more human. And we come to learn that, on another plane, even hearts hardened by cynicism or injustice or unwillingness to forgive are never beyond the reach of God, can always be opened to a new way of being, a vision of peace.

I exhort you all to pray every day for our world. And today I want to ask you to take up a specific task: please pray for me every day of my pilgrimage, for my own spiritual renewal in the Lord, and for the conversion of hearts to God's way of forgiveness and solidarity so that my hope—our hope—for unity and peace in the world will bear abundant fruit.

May God bless each of you and your families, and the teachers, caregivers, administrators, and benefactors of this center, and may Our Lady, Queen of Peace, protect you and guide you along the pilgrim-way of her Son, the Good Shepherd. Thank you for your attention.

Day Two

May 9, 2009

4

VISIT TO THE ANCIENT BASILICA OF THE MEMORIAL OF MOSES ON MOUNT NEBO

Father Minister General,
Father Custos,
Dear Friends,

In this holy place, consecrated by the memory of Moses, I greet all of you with affection in our Lord Jesus Christ. I thank Father José Rodríguez Carballo for his warm words of welcome. I also take this occasion to renew my gratitude, and that of the whole Church, to the Friars Minor of the Custody for their age-old presence in these lands, their joyful fidelity to the charism of Saint Francis, and their generous concern for the spiritual and material welfare of the local Christian communities and the countless pilgrims who visit the Holy Land each year. Here I wish to remember also, with particular gratitude, the late Father Michele Piccirillo, who devoted his life to the study of Christian antiquity and is buried in this shrine which was so dear to him.

It is appropriate that my pilgrimage should begin on this mountain, where Moses contemplated the Promised Land from afar. The magnificent prospect that opens up from the esplanade of this shrine invites us to ponder how that prophetic vision mysteriously embraced the great plan of salvation that God had prepared for his people. For it was in the valley of the Jordan, which stretches out below us, that in the fullness of time John the Baptist would come to prepare the way of the Lord. It was in the waters of the River Jordan that Jesus, after his baptism by John, would be revealed as the beloved Son of the Father and, anointed by the Holy Spirit, would inaugurate his public ministry. And it was from the Jordan that the Gospel would first go forth in Christ's own preaching and miracles, and then, after his resurrection and the descent of the Spirit at Pentecost, be brought by his disciples to the very ends of the earth.

Here, on the heights of Mount Nebo, the memory of Moses invites us to "lift up our eyes" to embrace with gratitude not only God's mighty works in the past, but also to look with faith and hope to the future that he holds out to us and to our world. Like Moses, we too have been called by name, invited to undertake a daily exodus from sin and slavery toward life and freedom, and given an unshakeable promise to guide our journey. In the waters of baptism, we have passed from the slavery of sin to new life and hope. In the communion of the Church, Christ's Body, we look forward to the vision of the heavenly city, the new Jerusalem, where God will be all in all. From this holy mountain, Moses directs our gaze on high, to the fulfillment of all God's promises in Christ.

Moses gazed upon the Promised Land from afar, at the end of his earthly pilgrimage. His example reminds us that we too are part of the ageless pilgrimage of God's people through history. In the footsteps of the prophets, the apostles, and the saints, we are called to walk with the Lord, to carry on his mission, to bear witness to the Gospel of God's universal love and mercy. We are called to welcome the coming of Christ's Kingdom by our charity, our service to the poor, and our efforts to be a leaven of reconciliation, forgiveness, and peace in the world around us. We know that, like Moses, we may not see the complete fulfillment of God's plan in our lifetime. Yet we trust that, by doing our small part in fidelity to the vocation each of us has received, we will help to make straight the paths of the Lord and welcome the dawn of his Kingdom. And we know that the God who revealed his name to Moses as a pledge that he would always be at our side (cf. Exod 3:14) will give us the strength to persevere in joyful hope even amid suffering, trial, and tribulation.

From the earliest times, Christians have come on pilgrimage to the sites linked to the history of the Chosen People, the events of Christ's life, and the nascent Church. This great tradition—which my present pilgrimage is meant to continue and confirm—is grounded in the desire to see, to touch, and to savor in prayer and contemplation the places blessed by the physical presence of our Savior, his Blessed Mother, the apostles, and the first disciples who saw him risen from the dead. Here, in the footsteps of the countless pilgrims who have preceded us in every century, we are challenged to appreciate more fully the gift of our faith and to grow in that communion which transcends every limit of language, race and culture.

The ancient tradition of pilgrimage to the holy places also reminds us of the inseparable bond between the Church and the Jewish people. From the beginning, the Church in these lands has commemorated in her liturgy the great figures of the patriarchs and prophets, as a sign of her profound appreciation of the unity of the two Testaments. May our encounter today inspire in us a renewed love for the canon of Sacred Scripture and a desire to overcome all obstacles to the reconciliation of Christians and Jews in mutual respect and cooperation in the service of that peace to which the word of God calls us!

Dear friends, gathered in this holy place, let us now raise our eyes and our hearts to the Father. As we prepare to pray the prayer which Jesus taught us, let us beg him to hasten the coming of his Kingdom so that we may see the fulfillment of his saving plan. And may we experience, with Saint Francis and all those pilgrims who have gone before us marked with the sign of faith, the gift of untold peace—*pax et bonum*—which awaits us in the heavenly Jerusalem.

5

BLESSING OF THE CORNERSTONE OF MADABA UNIVERSITY OF THE LATIN PATRIARCHATE

Dear Brother Bishops,
Dear Friends,

It is for me a great joy to bless this foundation stone of the University of Madaba. I thank His Beatitude Archbishop Fouad Twal, Latin Patriarch of Jerusalem, for his kind words of welcome. I wish to extend a special greeting of recognition to His Beatitude, Emeritus Patriarch Michel Sabbah, to whose initiative and efforts, together with those of Bishop Salim Sayegh, this new institution owes so much. I also greet the civil authorities, the bishops, priests, religious, and faithful, and all who accompany us for this important ceremony.

The Kingdom of Jordan has rightly given priority to the task of extending and improving education. I am aware that in this noble mission Her Majesty Queen Rania is especially active and her commitment is an inspiration to many. As I pay tribute to the efforts of so many people of goodwill committed to education, I note with satisfaction the competent and expert participation of Christian institutions, especially Catholic and Orthodox, in this overall effort. It is against this background that the Catholic Church, with the support of the Jordanian authorities, has sought to further university education in this country and elsewhere. This present initiative also responds to the request of many families who, pleased with the formation received in schools run by religious authorities, are demanding an analogous option at the university level.

I commend the promoters of this new institution for their courageous confidence in good education as a stepping-stone for personal development and for peace and progress in the region. In this context, the University of Madaba will surely keep in mind three important objectives. By developing the talents and noble attitudes of successive generations of students, it will prepare them to serve the wider community and help raise its living standards. By transmitting knowledge and instilling in students a love of truth, it will greatly enhance their adherence to sound values and their personal freedom. Finally, this same intellectual formation will sharpen their critical skills, dispel ignorance and prejudice, and assist in breaking the spell cast by ideologies old and new. The result of this process will be a university that is not only a platform for consolidating adherence to truth and to the values of a given culture, but a place of understanding and dialogue. While assimilating their own heritage, young Jordanians and other students from the region will be led to a deeper knowledge of human cultural achievements, will be enriched by other viewpoints, and will be formed in comprehension, tolerance, and peace.

This broader education is what one expects from institutions of higher learning and from their cultural milieu, be it secular or religious. In fact, belief in God does not suppress the search for truth; on the contrary, it encourages it. Saint Paul exhorted the early Christians to open their minds to "all that is true, all that is noble, all that is good and pure, all that we love and honor, all that is considered excellent or worthy of praise" (Phil 4:8). Religion, of course—like science and technology, philosophy and all expressions of our search for truth—can be corrupted. Religion is disfigured when pressed into the service of ignorance, prejudice, contempt, violence, and abuse. In this case, we see not only a perversion of religion but also a corruption of human freedom, a narrowing and blindness of the mind. Clearly, such an outcome is not inevitable. Indeed, when we promote education, we proclaim our confidence in the gift of freedom. The human heart can be hardened by the limits of its environment, by interests and passions. But every person is also called to wisdom and integrity, to the basic and all-important choice of good over evil, truth over dishonesty, and can be assisted in this task.

The call to moral integrity is perceived by the genuinely religious person, since the God of truth and love and beauty cannot be served in any other way. Mature belief in God serves greatly to guide the acquisition and proper application of knowledge. Science and technology offer extraordinary benefits to society and have greatly improved the quality of life of many human beings. Undoubtedly this is one of the hopes of those who are promoting this university, whose motto is *Sapientia et Scientia*. At the same time, the sciences have their limitations. They cannot answer all the questions about man and his existence. Indeed the human person: his place and purpose in the universe cannot be contained within the confines of science. "Humanity's intellectual nature finds its perfection ultimately in wisdom, which gently draws the human mind to seek and to love what is true and good" (cf.

Gaudium et Spes, 15). The use of scientific knowledge needs the guiding light of ethical wisdom. Such is the wisdom that inspired the Hippocratic oath, the 1948 Universal Declaration of Human Rights, the Geneva Convention, and other laudable international codes of conduct. Hence, religious and ethical wisdom, by answering questions of meaning and value, plays a central role in professional formation. And consequently, those universities where the quest for truth goes hand in hand with the search for what is good and noble offer an indispensable service to society.

With these thoughts in mind, I encourage in a special way the Christian students of Jordan and the neighboring regions to dedicate themselves responsibly to a proper professional and moral formation. You are called to be builders of a just and peaceful society composed of peoples of various religious and ethnic backgrounds. These realities—I wish to stress once more—must lead, not to division, but to mutual enrichment. The mission and the vocation of the University of Madaba is precisely to help you participate more fully in this noble task.

Dear friends, I wish to renew my congratulations to the Latin Patriarchate of Jerusalem and my encouragement to all who have taken this project to heart, together with those who are already engaged in the educational apostolate in this nation. May the Lord bless you and sustain you. I pray that your dreams may soon come true, that you may see generations of qualified men and women, Christian, Muslim, and of other religions, taking their place in society, equipped with professional skills, knowledgeable in their field, and educated in the values of wisdom, integrity, tolerance, and peace. Upon you and upon all the future students and staff of this university and their families, I invoke Almighty God's abundant blessings! Thank you!

6

MEETING WITH MUSLIM RELIGIOUS LEADERS, MEMBERS OF THE DIPLOMATIC CORPS, AND RECTORS OF UNIVERSITIES IN JORDAN, AT THE MOSQUE AL-HUSSEIN BIN TALAL, AMMAN

Your Royal Highness,
Your Excellencies,
Distinguished Ladies and Gentlemen,

It is a source of great joy for me to meet with you this morning in this magnificent setting. I wish to thank Prince Ghazi Bin Muhammad Bin Talal for his kind words of welcome. Your Royal Highness's numerous initiatives to promote interreligious and intercultural dialogue and exchanges are appreciated by the people of the Hashemite Kingdom and are widely respected by the international community. I know that these efforts receive the active support of other members of the royal family as well as the nation's government and find ample resonance in the many initiatives of collaboration among Jordanians. For all this, I wish to express my own heartfelt admiration.

Places of worship, like this splendid Al-Hussein Bin Talal mosque, named after the revered late king, stand out like jewels across the earth's surface. From the ancient to the modern, the magnificent to the humble, they all point to the Divine, to the Transcendent One, to the Almighty. And through the centuries these sanctuaries have drawn men and women into their sacred space to pause, to pray, to acknowledge the presence of the Almighty, and to recognize that we are all his creatures.

For this reason, we cannot fail to be concerned that today, with increasing insistency, some maintain that religion fails in its claim to be, by nature, a builder of unity and harmony, an expression of communion between persons and with God. Indeed, some assert that religion is necessarily a cause of division in our world; and so they argue that the less attention given to religion in the public sphere the better. Certainly, the contradiction of tensions and divisions between the followers of different religious traditions, sadly, cannot be denied. However, is it not also the case that often it is the ideological manipulation of religion, sometimes for political ends, that is the real catalyst for tension and division and, at times, even violence in society? In the face of this situation, where the opponents of religion seek not simply to silence its voice but to replace it with their own, the need for believers to be true to their principles and beliefs is felt all the more keenly. Muslims and Christians, precisely because of the burden of our common history so often marked by misunderstanding, must today strive to be known and recognized as worshippers of God faithful to prayer, eager to uphold and live by the Almighty's decrees, merciful and compassionate, consistent in bearing witness to all that is true and good, and ever mindful of the common origin and dignity of all human persons, who remain at the apex of God's creative design for the world and for history.

The resolve of Jordanian educators and religious and civic leaders to ensure that the public face of religion reflects its true nature is praiseworthy. The example of individuals and communities, together with the provision of courses and programs, manifest the constructive contribution of religion to the educational, cultural, social, and charitable sectors of your civic society. Some of this spirit I have been able to sample at first hand. Yesterday, I experienced the renowned educational and rehabilitation work of the Our Lady of Peace Center, where Christians and Muslims are transforming the lives of entire families, by assisting them to ensure that their disabled children take up their rightful place in society. Earlier this morning, I blessed the foundation stone of Madaba University, where young Muslim and Christian adults will side by side receive the benefits of a tertiary education, enabling them to contribute justly to the social and economic development of their nation. Of great merit too are the numerous initiatives of interreligious dialogue supported by the royal family and the diplomatic community, sometimes undertaken in conjunction with the Pontifical Council for Interreligious Dialogue. These include the ongoing work of the Royal Institute for Inter-faith Studies, the Royal Institute for Islamic Thought, the Amman Message of 2004, the Amman Interfaith Message of 2005, and the more recent Common Word letter, which echoed a theme consonant with my first encyclical: the unbreakable bond between love of God and love of neighbor, and the fundamental contradiction of resorting to violence or exclusion in the name of God (cf. *Deus Caritas Est*, 16).

Such initiatives clearly lead to greater reciprocal knowledge, and they foster a growing respect both for what we hold in common and for what we understand differently. Thus, they should prompt Christians and Muslims to probe even more deeply the essential relationship between God and his world so that together we may strive to ensure that society resonates in harmony with the divine order. In this regard, the cooperation found here in Jordan sets an encouraging and persuasive example for the region, and indeed the world, of the positive, creative contribution that religion can and must make to civic society.

Distinguished friends, today I wish to refer to a task which I have addressed on a number of occasions and which I firmly believe Christians and Muslims can embrace, particularly through our respective contributions to learning, scholarship, and public service. That task is the challenge to cultivate for the good, in the context of faith and truth, the vast potential of human reason. Christians in fact describe God, among other ways, as creative Reason, which orders and guides the world. And God endows us with the capacity to participate in his Reason and thus to act in accordance with what is good. Muslims worship God, the Creator of Heaven and Earth, who has spoken to humanity. And as believers in the one God, we both know that human reason is itself God's gift and that it soars to its highest plane when suffused with the light of God's truth. In fact, when human reason humbly allows itself to be purified by faith, it is far from weakened; rather, it is strengthened to resist presumption and to reach beyond its own limitations. In this way, human reason is emboldened to pursue its noble purpose of serving mankind, giving expression to our deepest common aspirations, and extending, rather than manipulating or confining, public debate. Thus, genuine adherence to religion—far from narrowing our minds—widens the horizon of human understanding. Genuine adherence to religion protects civil society from the excesses of the unbridled ego, which tend to absolutize the finite and to eclipse the infinite; it ensures that freedom is exercised hand in hand with truth; and it adorns culture with insights concerning all that is true, good, and beautiful.

This understanding of reason, which continually draws the human mind beyond itself in the quest for the Absolute,

poses a challenge; it contains a sense of both hope and cau-
tion. Together, Christians and Muslims are impelled to seek
all that is just and right. We are bound to step beyond our
particular interests and to encourage others—in particular,
civil servants and leaders—to do likewise, in order to
embrace the profound satisfaction of serving the common
good, even at personal cost. And we are reminded that
because it is our common human dignity which gives rise to
universal human rights, they hold equally for every man and
woman, irrespective of his or her religious, social, or ethnic
group. In this regard, we must note that the right of religious
freedom extends beyond the question of worship and
includes the right—especially of minorities—to fair access to
the employment market and other spheres of civic life.

Before I leave you this morning I would like to
acknowledge in a special way the presence among us of His
Beatitude Emmanuel III Delly, Patriarch of Baghdad, whom
I greet most warmly. His presence brings to mind the people
of neighboring Iraq, many of whom have found welcome
refuge here in Jordan. The international community's efforts
to promote peace and reconciliation, together with those of
the local leaders, must continue in order to bear fruit in the
lives of Iraqis. I wish to express my appreciation for all those
who are assisting in the endeavors to deepen trust and to
rebuild the institutions and infrastructures essential to the
well-being of that society. And once again, I urge diplomats
and the international community they represent, together
with local political and religious leaders, to do everything
possible to ensure the ancient Christian community of that
noble land its fundamental right to peaceful coexistence with
their fellow citizens.

Distinguished friends, I trust that the sentiments I have
expressed today will leave us with renewed hope for the

future. Our love and duty before the Almighty is expressed not only in our worship but also in our love and concern for children and young people—your families—and for all Jordanians. It is for them that you labor and it is they who motivate you to place the good of every human person at the heart of institutions, laws, and the workings of society. May reason, ennobled and humbled by the grandeur of God's truth, continue to shape the life and institutions of this nation, in order that families may flourish and that all may live in peace, contributing to and drawing upon the culture that unifies this great kingdom! Thank you very much!

7

CELEBRATION OF VESPERS WITH PRIESTS, MEN AND WOMEN RELIGIOUS, SEMINARIANS, AND ECCLESIAL MOVEMENTS, IN THE GREEK-MELKITE CATHEDRAL OF SAINT-GEORGES, AMMAN

Dear Brothers and Sisters,

It is a great joy for me to celebrate Vespers with you this evening in the Greek-Melkite Cathedral of Saint George. I warmly greet His Beatitude Gregorios III Laham, the Greek Melkite Patriarch, who has joined us from Damascus; as well as Emeritus Archbishop Georges El-Murr and His Excellency Yaser Ayyach, Archbishop of Petra and Philadelphia, whom I thank for his kind words of welcome, which I gladly reciprocate with sentiments of respect. I also greet the leaders of the other Catholic Churches present in the East—Maronite, Syrian, Armenian, Chaldean, and Latin. To all of you and to the priests, sisters and brothers, seminarians and lay faithful, gathered here this evening, I express my sincere thanks for giving me this opportunity to pray with you and to experience something of the richness of our liturgical traditions.

The Church herself is a pilgrim people and thus, through the centuries, has been marked by determinant historical events and pervading cultural epochs. Sadly, some of these have included times of theological dispute or periods of repression. Others, however, have been moments of reconciliation—marvelously strengthening the communion of the Church—and times of rich cultural revival, to which Eastern Christians have contributed so greatly. Particular Churches within the universal Church attest to the dynamism of her earthly journey and manifest to all members of the faithful a treasure of spiritual, liturgical, and ecclesiastical traditions that point to God's universal goodness and his will, seen throughout history, to draw all into his divine life.

The ancient living treasure of the traditions of the Eastern Churches enriches the universal Church and could never be understood simply as objects to be passively preserved. All Christians are called to respond actively to the Lord's mandate—as Saint George did in dramatic ways, according to popular record—to bring others to know and to love him. In fact, the vicissitudes of history have strengthened the members of particular Churches to embrace this task with vigor and to engage resolutely with the pastoral realities of today. Most of you trace ancient links to the Patriarchate of Antioch, and your communities are thus rooted here in the Near East. And, just as two thousand years ago it was in Antioch that the disciples were first called Christians, so also today, as small minorities in scattered communities across these lands, you too are recognized as followers of the Lord. The public face of your Christian faith is certainly not restricted to the spiritual solicitude you bear for one another and your people, essential though that is. Rather, your many works of universal charity extend to all Jordanians—Muslims and those of other religions—and also to the large numbers of refugees whom this kingdom so generously welcomes.

Dear brothers and sisters, Psalm 103 that we prayed this evening presents us with glorious images of God the bountiful Creator, actively present in his creation, providing life with abundant goodness and wise order, ever ready to renew the face of the earth! The Epistle reading we have just heard, however, paints a different picture. It warns us, not in a threatening way, but realistically, of the need to stay alert, to be aware of the forces of evil at work creating darkness in our world (cf. Eph 6:10–20). Some might be tempted to think this a contradiction; yet, reflecting on our ordinary human experience, we recognize spiritual struggle; we acknowledge the daily need to move into Christ's light, to choose life, to seek truth. Indeed, this rhythm—turning away from evil and girding ourselves with the Lord's strength—is what we celebrate at every baptism, the gateway to Christian life, the first step along the way of the Lord's disciples. Recalling Christ's baptism by John in the waters of the Jordan, the assembled pray that the one to be baptized will be rescued from the kingdom of darkness and brought into the splendor of God's kingdom of light, and so receive the gift of new life.

This dynamic movement from death to newness of life, from darkness to light, from despair to hope that we experience so dramatically during the Triduum, and that is celebrated with great joy in the season of Easter, ensures that the

Church herself remains young. She is alive because Christ is alive, truly risen. Vivified by the presence of the Spirit, she reaches out every day, drawing men and women to the living Lord. Dear bishops, priests, brothers and sisters, dear lay faithful: our respective roles of service and mission within the Church are the tireless response of a pilgrim people. Your liturgies, ecclesiastical discipline, and spiritual heritage are a living witness to your unfolding tradition. You amplify the echo of the first Gospel proclamation, you render fresh the ancient memories of the works of the Lord, you make present his saving graces, and you diffuse anew the first glimmers of the Easter light and the flickering flames of Pentecost.

In this way, imitating Christ and the Old Testament patriarchs and prophets, we set out to lead people from the desert toward the place of life, toward the Lord who gives us life in abundance. This marks all your apostolic works, the variety and caliber of which are greatly appreciated. From kindergartens to places of higher education; from orphanages to homes for the elderly; from work with refugees to a music academy, medical clinics and hospitals, interreligious dialogue, and cultural initiatives—your presence in this society is a marvelous sign of the hope that defines us as Christian.

That hope reaches far beyond the confines of our own Christian communities. So often you find that the families of other religions, with whom you work and offer your service of universal charity, hold concerns and worries that cross religious and cultural boundaries. This is especially noticeable in regard to the hopes and aspirations of parents for their children. What parent or person of goodwill could not be troubled by the negative influences so pervasive in our globalized world, including the destructive elements within the entertainment industry that so callously exploit the innocence and sensibility of the vulnerable and the young? Yet, with your eyes firmly fixed on Christ, the light who dispels all evil, restores lost innocence, and humbles earthly pride, you will sustain a magnificent vision of hope for all those you meet and serve.

May I conclude with a special word of encouragement to those present who are in formation for the priesthood and religious life. Guided by the light of the Risen Lord, inflamed with his hope, and vested with his truth and love, your witness will bring abundant blessings to those whom you meet along the way. Indeed the same holds for all young Christian Jordanians: do not be afraid to make your own wise, measured, and respectful contribution to the public life of the Kingdom. The authentic voice of faith will always bring integrity, justice, compassion, and peace!

Dear friends, with sentiments of great respect for all of you gathered with me this evening in worship, I again thank you for your prayers for my ministry as the Successor of Peter, and I assure you and all those entrusted to your pastoral care of a remembrance in my own daily prayer.

Thank you.

Day Three

May 10, 2009

8

HOMILY AT MASS CELEBRATED AT THE AMMAN INTERNATIONAL STADIUM

Fourth Sunday of Easter

Dear Brothers and Sisters in Christ,

I rejoice that we are able to celebrate this Eucharist together at the beginning of my pilgrimage to the Holy Land. Yesterday, from the heights of Mount Nebo, I stood and looked out upon this great land, the land of Moses, Elijah, and John the Baptist, the land where God's ancient promises were fulfilled in the coming of the Messiah, Jesus our Lord. This land witnessed his preaching and miracles, his death and resurrection, and the outpouring of the Holy Spirit upon the Church, the sacrament of a reconciled and renewed humanity. As I pondered the mystery of God's fidelity, I prayed that the Church in these lands would be confirmed in hope and strengthened in her witness to the Risen Christ, the Savior of mankind. Truly, as Saint Peter tells us in today's first reading, "There is no other name under heaven given among men by which we are to be saved" (Acts 4:12).

Today's joyful celebration of the Eucharistic sacrifice expresses the rich diversity of the Catholic Church in the Holy Land. I greet all of you with affection in the Lord. I thank His Beatitude Fouad Twal, Latin Patriarch of

Jerusalem, for his kind words of welcome. My greeting goes also to the many young people from Catholic schools who today bring their enthusiasm to this Eucharistic celebration.

In the Gospel that we have just heard, Jesus proclaims: "I am the good shepherd…who lays down his life for the sheep" (John 10:11). As the Successor of Saint Peter, to whom the Lord entrusted the care of his flock (cf. John 21:15–17), I have long awaited this opportunity to stand before you as a witness to the Risen Savior, and to encourage you to persevere in faith, hope and love, in fidelity to the ancient traditions and the distinguished history of Christian witness which you trace back to the age of the Apostles. The Catholic community here is deeply touched by the difficulties and uncertainties which affect all the people of the Middle East. May you never forget the great dignity that derives from your Christian heritage or fail to sense the loving solidarity of all your brothers and sisters in the Church throughout the world!

"I am the good shepherd," the Lord tells us. "I know my own, and my own know me" (John 10:14). Today in Jordan we celebrate the World Day of Prayer for Vocations. As we reflect on the Gospel of the Good Shepherd, let us ask the Lord to open our hearts and minds ever more fully to hear his call. Truly, Jesus "knows us," even more deeply than we know ourselves, and he has a plan for each one of us. We know, too, that wherever he calls us, we will find happiness and fulfillment; indeed, we will find our very selves (cf. Matt 10:39). Today I invite the many young people here present to consider how the Lord is calling you to follow him and to build up his Church. Whether it be in the priestly ministry, in consecrated life, or in the sacrament of marriage, Jesus needs you to make his voice heard and to work for the growth of his Kingdom.

In today's second reading, Saint John invites us to "think of the love that the Father has lavished on us" by making us

Jamal Saidi/REUTERS

Pope Benedict XVI waves to the faithful during Sunday Mass in Amman.

his adopted children in Christ. Hearing these words should make us grateful for the experience of the Father's love which we have had in our families, from the love of our fathers and mothers, our grandparents, our brothers and sisters. During the celebration of the present Year of the Family, the Church throughout the Holy Land has reflected on the family as a mystery of life-giving love, endowed in God's plan with its own proper calling and mission: to radiate the divine Love which is the source and the ultimate fulfillment of all the other loves of our lives. May every Christian family grow in fidelity to its lofty vocation to be a true school of prayer, where children learn a sincere love of God, where they mature in self-discipline and concern for the needs of others, and where, shaped by the wisdom born of faith, they contribute to the building of an ever more-just and fraternal society. The strong Christian families of these lands are a great legacy handed down from earlier generations. May today's families be faithful to that impressive heritage, and never lack the material and moral assistance they need to carry out their irreplaceable role in service to society.

An important aspect of your reflection during this Year of the Family has been the particular dignity, vocation, and mission of women in God's plan. How much the Church in these lands owes to the patient, loving, and faithful witness of countless Christian mothers, religious sisters, teachers, doctors, and nurses! How much your society owes to all those women who in different and at times courageous ways have devoted their lives to building peace and fostering love! From the very first pages of the Bible, we see how man and woman, created in the image of God, are meant to complement one another as stewards of God's gifts and as partners in communicating his gift of life, both physical and spiritual, to our world. Sadly, this God-given dignity and role of women has not always been sufficiently understood and esteemed. The Church, and society as a whole, has come to realize how urgently we need what the late Pope John Paul II called the "prophetic charism" of women (cf. *Mulieris Dignitatem*, 29) as bearers of love, teachers of mercy, and artisans of peace, bringing warmth and humanity to a world that all too often judges the value of a person by the cold criteria of usefulness and profit. By its public witness of respect for women, and its defense of the innate dignity of every human person, the Church in the Holy Land can make an important contribution to the advancement of a culture of true humanity and the building of the civilization of love.

Dear friends, let us return to the words of Jesus in today's Gospel. I believe that they contain a special message for you, his faithful flock in these lands where he once dwelt. "The good shepherd," he tells us, "lays down his life for his sheep." At the beginning of this Mass, we asked the Father to "give us new strength from the courage of Christ our shepherd," who remained steadfast, in fidelity to the Father's will (Opening Prayer, Mass of the Fourth Sunday of Easter). May the courage of Christ our Shepherd inspire and sustain you daily in your efforts to bear witness to the Christian faith and to maintain the Church's presence in the changing social fabric of these ancient lands.

Fidelity to your Christian roots, fidelity to the Church's mission in the Holy Land, demands of each of you a particular kind of courage: the courage of conviction, born of personal faith, not mere social convention or family tradition; the courage to engage in dialogue and to work side by side with other Christians in the service of the Gospel and solidarity with the poor, the displaced, and the victims of profound human tragedies; the courage to build new bridges to enable a fruitful encounter of people of different religions and cultures, and thus to enrich the fabric of society. It also means bearing witness to the love that inspires us to "lay down" our lives in the service of others, and thus to counter ways of thinking which justify "taking" innocent lives.

"I am the good shepherd; I know my own, and my own know me" (John 10:14). Rejoice that the Lord has made you members of his flock and knows each of you by name! Follow him with joy and let him guide you in all your ways. Jesus knows what challenges you face, what trials you endure, and the good that you do in his name. Trust in him and in his enduring love for all the members of his flock, and persevere in your witness to the triumph of his love. May Saint John the Baptist, the patron of Jordan, and Mary, Virgin and Mother, sustain you by their example and prayers, and lead you to the fullness of joy in the eternal pastures where we will experience for ever the presence of the Good Shepherd and know forever the depths of his love. Amen.

9

REGINA COELI OFFERED AT THE AMMAN INTERNATIONAL STADIUM

Dear Friends,

During the Mass, I spoke about the prophetic charism of women as bearers of love, teachers of mercy, and artisans of peace. The supreme example of womanly virtue is the Blessed Virgin Mary: the Mother of Mercy and Queen of Peace. As we turn to her now, let us seek her maternal intercession for all the families of these lands, that they may truly be schools of prayer and schools of love. Let us ask the Mother of the Church to look down in mercy upon all the Christians of these lands, and, with the help of her prayers, may they be truly one in the faith they profess and the witness they bear. Let us ask her who responded so generously to the angel's call, and who accepted her vocation to become the Mother of God, to give courage and strength to all young people today who are discerning their vocations, so that they too may generously dedicate themselves to carrying out the Lord's will.

In this season of Eastertide, it is with the title *Regina Coeli* that we call upon the Blessed Virgin. As a fruit of the redemption won by her Son's death and resurrection, she too was raised to everlasting glory and crowned Queen of Heaven. With great confidence in the power of her intercession, with joy in our hearts, and with love for our glorious ever-Virgin Mother, we turn to her now and ask for her prayers.

10

BLESSING OF THE FOUNDATION STONES OF THE LATIN AND GREEK MELKITE CHURCHES AT BETHANY BEYOND THE JORDAN

Your Royal Highness,
Dear Brother Bishops,
Dear Friends,

It is with great spiritual joy that I come to bless the foundation stones of two Catholic Churches to be built beside the River Jordan, a place marked by many memorable events in biblical history. The prophet Elijah the Tishbite was from this area, not far north of Galaad. Near here, facing Jericho, the waters of the Jordan opened before Elijah, who was taken up by the Lord in a chariot of fire (cf. 2 Kgs 2:9–12). Here the Spirit of the Lord called John the son of Zechariah to preach a conversion of hearts. John the Evangelist also places in this area the meeting between the Baptist and Jesus, who at his baptism was "anointed" by the Spirit of God descending as a dove and was proclaimed the beloved Son of the Father (cf. John 1:28; Mark 1:9–11).

I was honored to be received at this important site by Their Majesties King Abdullah II and Queen Rania. I again wish to express my sincere gratitude for the warm hospitality they have shown me during my visit to the Hashemite Kingdom of Jordan. I greet with joy His Beatitude Gregorios III Laham, Patriarch of Antioch for the Greek Melkite Church. I also greet with affection His Beatitude Fouad Twal,

Latin Patriarch of Jerusalem. I extend my warm best wishes to His Beatitude Michel Sabbah, to the auxiliary bishops present, particularly to Archbishop Yasser Ayyach and the Most Reverend Salim Sayegh, whom I thank for his kind words of welcome. I am pleased to greet all the bishops, priests, religious, and faithful who accompany us today. Let us rejoice in the knowledge that the two buildings, one Latin, the other Greek Melkite, will serve to build up, each according to the traditions of its own community, the one family of God.

The foundation stone of a church is a symbol of Christ. The Church rests on Christ, is sustained by him, and cannot be separated from him. He is the one foundation of every Christian community, the living stone, rejected by the builders but chosen and precious in God's sight as the cornerstone (cf. 1 Pet 2:4–5, 7). With him, we too are living stones built into a spiritual house, a dwelling place for God (cf. Eph 2:20–22; 1 Pet 2:5). Saint Augustine loved to refer to the mystery of the Church as the *Christus totus*, the whole Christ, the full or complete Body of Christ—Head and members. This is the reality of the Church: it is Christ and us, Christ with us. He is with us as the vine is with its own branches (cf. John 15:1–8). The Church is in Christ a community of new life, a dynamic reality of grace that flows from him. Through the Church Christ purifies our hearts, enlightens our minds, unites us with the Father, and, in the one Spirit, moves us to a daily exercise of Christian love. We confess this joyful reality as the one, holy, catholic, and apostolic Church.

We enter the Church through baptism. The memory of Christ's own baptism is brought vividly before us in this place. Jesus stood in line with sinners and accepted John's baptism of penance as a prophetic sign of his own passion, death, and resurrection for the forgiveness of sins. Down through the centuries, many pilgrims have come to the Jordan to seek purification, renew their faith, and draw closer to the Lord. Such was the pilgrim Egeria, who left a written account of her visit during the late fourth century. The sacrament of baptism, drawing its power from Christ's death and resurrection, will be cherished especially by the Christian communities that gather in the new church buildings. May the Jordan always remind you that you have been washed in the waters of baptism and have become members of the family of Jesus. Your lives, in obedience to his word, are being transformed into his image and likeness. As you strive to be faithful to your baptismal commitment of conversion, witness, and mission, know that you are being strengthened by the gift of the Holy Spirit.

Dear brothers and sisters, may the prayerful contemplation of these mysteries enrich you with spiritual joy and moral courage. With the Apostle Paul, I encourage you to grow in the whole range of noble attitudes covered by the blessed name of agape, Christian love (cf. 1 Cor 13:1–13). Promote dialogue and understanding in civil society, especially when claiming your legitimate rights. In the Middle East, marked by tragic suffering, by years of violence and unresolved tensions, Christians are called to offer their contribution, inspired by the example of Jesus, of reconciliation and peace through forgiveness and generosity. Continue being grateful to those who lead you and who serve you faithfully as ministers of Christ. You do well to accept their guidance in faith knowing that, by receiving the apostolic teaching they transmit, you welcome Christ and you welcome the One who sent him (cf. Matt 10:40).

My dear brothers and sisters, we now proceed to bless these two stones, the beginning of two new sacred buildings. May the Lord sustain, strengthen, and increase the communities that will worship in them. And may he bless you all with his gift of peace. Amen!

Day Four

May 11, 2009

11

FAREWELL CEREMONY AT QUEEN ALIA INTERNATIONAL AIRPORT, AMMAN

Your Majesties,
Your Excellencies,
Dear Friends,

As I prepare for the next stage of my pilgrimage to the lands of the Bible, I want to thank all of you for the warm welcome that I have received in Jordan over these last few days. I thank His Majesty King Abdullah II for inviting me to visit the Hashemite Kingdom, for his hospitality and his kind words. I also express my appreciation for the immense effort that has gone into making my visit possible, and ensuring the orderly unfolding of the various meetings and celebrations that have taken place. The public authorities, assisted by a great number of volunteers, have worked long and hard in order to direct the crowds and organize the different events. The media coverage has enabled countless people to follow the celebrations even if they could not be physically present. As well as thanking those who have made this possible, I wish to extend a special greeting to all who are listening on the radio or watching on television, especially the sick and those confined to their homes.

It has been a particular joy for me to be present at the launching of a number of major initiatives promoted by the

Catholic community here in Jordan. The new wing of the Regina Pacis Center will open up fresh possibilities of bringing hope to those who struggle with difficulties of various kinds, and to their families. The two churches to be built in Bethany will enable their respective communities to welcome pilgrims and to foster the spiritual growth of all who worship in that holy place. The University at Madaba has a particularly important contribution to offer to the wider community, in forming young people from various traditions in the skills that will enable them to shape the future of civil society. To all who are involved in these projects, I offer good wishes and the promise of my prayers.

One of the highlights of these days was my visit to the Mosque Al-Hussein Bin Talal, where I had the pleasure of meeting Muslim religious leaders, together with members of the diplomatic corps and university rectors. I would like to encourage all Jordanians, whether Christian or Muslim, to build on the firm foundations of religious tolerance that enable the members of different communities to live together in peace and mutual respect. His Majesty the King has been notably active in fostering interreligious dialogue, and I want to put on record how much his commitment in this regard is appreciated. I also gratefully acknowledge the particular consideration that he shows toward the Christian community in Jordan. This spirit of openness not only helps the members of different ethnic communities in this country to live together in peace and concord, but it has contributed to Jordan's far-sighted political initiatives to build peace throughout the Middle East.

Dear friends, as you know, it is principally as a pilgrim and a pastor that I have come to Jordan. Hence, the experiences from these days that will remain most firmly etched in my memory are my visits to the holy places and the moments of prayer that we celebrated together. Once again I want to express the appreciation of the whole Church to those who look after the places of pilgrimage in this land, and I also thank the many people who contributed to the planning of Saturday's Vespers in Saint George's Cathedral and yesterday's Mass at the International Stadium. It was truly a joy for me to experience these Eastertide celebrations in company with the Catholic faithful from different traditions, united in the Church's communion, and in witness to Christ. I encourage all of them to remain faithful to their baptismal commitment, mindful that Christ himself received baptism from John in the waters of the River Jordan.

As I bid you farewell, I want you to know that I hold in my heart the people of the Hashemite Kingdom and all who live throughout this region. I pray that you may enjoy peace and prosperity, now and for generations to come. Thank you once again. And may God bless all of you!

12

WELCOMING CEREMONY AT BEN GURION INTERNATIONAL AIRPORT, TEL AVIV

Mr. President,
Mr. Prime Minister,
Your Excellencies,
Ladies, and Gentlemen,

Thank you for your warm welcome to the State of Israel, a land which is held holy by millions of believers around the world. I am grateful to the president, Mr. Shimon Peres, for his kind words, and I appreciate the opportunity that has been offered to me to come on pilgrimage to a land that is hallowed by the footsteps of patriarchs and prophets, a land that Christians hold in particular veneration as the setting for the events of the life, death, and resurrection of Jesus Christ. I take my place in a long line of Christian pilgrims to these shores, a line that stretches back to the earliest centuries of the Church's history and that, I am sure, will continue long into the future. I come, like so many others before me, to pray at the holy places, to pray especially for peace—peace here in the Holy Land, and peace throughout the world.

Mr. President, the Holy See and the State of Israel have many shared values, above all a commitment to give religion its rightful place in the life of society. The just ordering of social relationships presupposes and requires a respect for the freedom and dignity of every human being, whom Christians, Muslims, and Jews alike believe to be created by a loving God and destined for eternal life. When the religious dimension of the human person is denied or marginalized, the very foundation for a proper understanding of inalienable human rights is placed in jeopardy.

Tragically, the Jewish people have experienced the terrible consequences of ideologies that deny the fundamental dignity of every human person. It is right and fitting that, during my stay in Israel, I will have the opportunity to honor the memory of the six million Jewish victims of the Shoah, and to pray that humanity will never again witness a crime of such magnitude. Sadly, anti-Semitism continues to rear its ugly head in many parts of the world. This is totally unacceptable. Every effort must be made to combat anti-Semitism wherever it is found, and to promote respect and esteem for the members of every people, tribe, language, and nation across the globe.

During my stay in Jerusalem, I will have the pleasure of meeting many of this country's distinguished religious leaders. One thing that the three great monotheistic religions have in common is a special veneration for that holy city. It is my earnest hope that all pilgrims to the holy places will be able to access them freely and without restraint, to take part in religious ceremonies, and to promote the worthy upkeep of places of worship on sacred sites. May the words of Isaiah's prophecy be fulfilled, that many nations shall flow to the mountain of the house of the Lord, that he may teach them his ways, that they may walk in his paths—paths of peace and justice, paths that lead to reconciliation and harmony (cf. Isa 2:2–5).

Even though the name Jerusalem means "city of peace," it is all too evident that, for decades, peace has tragically eluded the inhabitants of this holy land. The eyes of the world are upon the peoples of this region as they struggle to achieve a just and lasting solution to conflicts that have caused so much suffering. The hopes of countless men, women, and children for a more secure and stable future depend on the outcome of negotiations for peace between Israelis and Palestinians. In union with people of goodwill everywhere, I plead with all those responsible to explore every possible avenue in the search for a just resolution of the outstanding difficulties, so that both peoples may live in peace in a homeland of their own, within secure and internationally recognized borders. In this regard, I hope and pray that a climate of greater trust can soon be created that will enable the parties to make real progress along the road to peace and stability.

To the Catholic bishops and faithful here present, I

offer a special word of greeting. In this land, where Peter received his commission to feed the Lord's sheep, I come as Peter's successor to minister among you. It will be my special joy to join you for the concluding celebrations of the Year of the Family, due to take place in Nazareth, home of the Holy Family of Jesus, Mary, and Joseph. As I said in my message for the World Day of Peace last year, the family is the "first and indispensable teacher of peace" (no. 3), and hence it has a vital role to play in healing divisions in human society at every level. To the Christian communities in the Holy Land, I say, By your faithful witness to him who preached forgiveness and reconciliation, by your commitment to uphold the sacredness of every human life, you can make a particular contribution to ending the hostilities that for so long have afflicted this land. I pray that your continuing presence in Israel and the Palestinian Territories will bear much fruit in promoting peace and mutual respect among all the peoples who live in the lands of the Bible.

Mr. President, ladies and gentlemen, once again I thank you for your welcome and I assure you of my sentiments of goodwill. May God give his people strength! May God bless his people with peace!

13

COURTESY VISIT TO
THE PRESIDENT OF THE
STATE OF ISRAEL

Presidential Palace, Jerusalem

Mr. President,
Your Excellencies,
Ladies and Gentlemen,

As a kind gesture of hospitality, President Peres has welcomed us here to his residence, enabling me to greet you all and to have this opportunity to share a few thoughts with you. Mr. President, I thank you for this gracious welcome, and for your courteous greeting which I warmly reciprocate. I also thank the singers and musicians who have entertained us with their fine performance.

Mr. President, in the message of congratulations that I sent to you on the occasion of your inauguration, I gladly recalled your distinguished record of public service marked by a strong commitment to the pursuit of justice and peace. This afternoon I wish to assure you and the new government, and all the people of the State of Israel, that my pilgrimage to the holy places is one of prayer for the precious gift of unity and peace for the Middle East and for all humanity. Indeed, I pray daily for a peace born of justice to return to the Holy Land and the entire region, bringing security and renewed hope for all.

Peace is above all a divine gift. For peace is the Almighty's promise to humanity, and it harbors unity. In the Book of the prophet Jeremiah we read: "I know the plans I have in mind for you—it is the Lord who speaks—plans for peace not disaster, to give you a future and a hope" (Jer 29:11–12). The prophet reminds us of the Almighty's promise that he can "be found," that he "will listen," that he "will gather us together as one." But there is a proviso: we must "seek him," and "seek him with all our heart" (cf. Jer 29: 12–14).

To the religious leaders present this afternoon, I wish to say that the particular contribution of religions to the quest for peace lies primarily in the wholehearted, united search for God. Ours is the task of proclaiming and witnessing that the Almighty is present and knowable even when he seems hidden from our sight, that he acts in our world for our good, and that a society's future is marked with hope when it resonates in harmony with his divine order. It is God's dynamic presence that draws hearts together and ensures unity. In fact, the ultimate foundation of unity among persons lies in the perfect oneness and universality of God, who created man and woman in his image and likeness in order to draw us into his own divine life so that all may be one.

Religious leaders must therefore be mindful that any division or tension, any tendency to introversion or suspicion among believers or between our communities, can easily lead to a contradiction that obscures the Almighty's oneness, betrays our unity, and contradicts the One who reveals himself as "abounding in steadfast love and faithfulness" (Exod 34:6; Ps 138:2; Ps 85:11). My friends, Jerusalem, which has long been a crossroads for peoples of many different origins, is a city that affords Jews, Christians, and Muslims both the duty and the privilege to bear witness together to the peaceful coexistence long desired by worshippers of the one God, to lay bare the Almighty's plan for the unity of the human family announced to Abraham, and

Ahikam Seri/REUTERS

Israel's President Shimon Peres gives a wreath of wheat to
Pope Benedict XVI during his official welcoming ceremony
at the presidential residence in Jerusalem.

to proclaim the true nature of man as a seeker of God. Let
us resolve to ensure that through the teaching and guidance
of our respective communities we shall assist them to be true
to who they are as believers, ever aware of the infinite goodness of God, the inviolable dignity of every human being,
and the unity of the entire human family.

Sacred Scripture also presents us with an understanding
of security. According to the Hebrew usage, security—*batah*—
arises from trust and refers not just to the absence of threat
but also to the sentiment of calmness and confidence. In the
Book of the prophet Isaiah we read of a time of divine blessing: "Once more the Spirit is poured upon us...and justice will
dwell in the wilderness and integrity in the fertile land;
integrity will bring peace, and justice everlasting security" (Isa
32:15–17). Security, integrity, justice, and peace. In God's
design for the world, these are inseparable. Far from being
simply products of human endeavor, they are values that stem

from God's fundamental relationship with man, and dwell as a common patrimony in the heart of every individual.

There is only one way to protect and promote these values: Exercise them! Live them! No individual, family, community, or nation is exempt from the duty to live in justice and to work for peace. And naturally, civic and political leaders are expected to ensure just and proper security for the people whom they have been elected to serve. That objective forms a part of the rightful promotion of values common to humanity and thus cannot conflict with the unity of the human family. The authentic values and goals of a society, which always safeguard human dignity, are indivisible, universal, and interdependent (cf. Address to the United Nations, 18 April 2008). Thus, they cannot be satisfied when they fall prey to particular interests or piecemeal politics. A nation's true interest is always served by the pursuit of justice for all.

Distinguished ladies and gentlemen, lasting security is a matter of trust, nurtured in justice and integrity, and sealed through the conversion of hearts that stirs us to look the other in the eye and to recognize the "Thou" as my equal, my brother, my sister. In this way, does not society itself become the "fruitful field" (Isa 32:15) marked, not by blocks or obstructions, but by cohesion and vibrancy? Can it not become a community with noble aspirations, where all are willingly afforded access to education, family housing, and the opportunity for employment, a society ready to build upon the lasting foundations of hope?

To conclude, I would like to turn to the ordinary families of this city, of this country. What parents would ever want violence, insecurity, or disunity for their son or daughter? What humane political end can ever be served through conflict and violence? I hear the cry of those who live in this land for justice, for peace, for respect for their dignity, for lasting security, for a daily life free from the fear of outside threats and senseless violence. And I know that considerable numbers of men and women and young people are working for peace and solidarity through cultural programs and through initiatives of compassionate and practical outreach; humble enough to forgive, they have the courage to grasp the dream that is their right.

Mr. President, I thank you for the courtesy you have shown to me and I assure you again of my prayers for the government and all the citizens of this State. May a genuine conversion of the hearts of all lead to an ever-strengthening commitment to peace and security through justice for everyone.

Shalom!

The following is a summary of the gestures and words of welcome that preceded the delivery of the formal address given above:

The Holy Father was greeted by three Israeli girls in English, Hebrew, and Arabic and invited to taste a fig representing the "fruits from the State of Israel." The young people also offered His Holiness a sheaf of wheat, developed at the Volcani Center of the Agricultural Research Organization, with the potential to produce a double yield. President Peres announced that this specially designed crop "contains an answer to starvation" and has been named after His Holiness.

His Excellency expressed his admiration for Pope Benedict as the spiritual leader of the Catholic Church. The President then thanked His Holiness for his address during the welcoming ceremony at Ben Gurion Airport. He spoke of his particular appreciation for the Holy Father's words in regard to the Holocaust, its victims, and anti-Semitism, saying that the speech "really aimed at the most difficult part of our life, the most penetrating problems."

The Holy Father expressed his happiness to be in Israel and his deep appreciation for the cordial welcome and for the presentation of the "Wheat of Pope Benedict XVI" and the other gifts. His Holiness reiterated his conviction that Israel is a land very important for peace throughout the world, highlighting that "your prophets are our prophets" and "your fathers are our fathers." In closing, the Holy Father expressed his hope that Christians and Jews would continue their efforts to understand one another as brothers and sisters, and so cooperate to promote peace throughout the world.

14

VISIT TO THE YAD VASHEM MEMORIAL

I will give in my house and within my walls a memorial and a name....I will give them an ever-lasting name which shall not be cut off. (Isa 56:5)

This passage from the Book of the prophet Isaiah furnishes the two simple words that solemnly express the profound significance of this revered place: *yad*—"memorial"; *shem*—"name." I have come to stand in silence before this monument, erected to honor the memory of the millions of Jews killed in the horrific tragedy of the Shoah. They lost their lives, but they will never lose their names: these are indelibly etched in the hearts of their loved ones, their surviving fellow prisoners, and all those determined never to allow such an atrocity to disgrace mankind again. Most of all, their names are forever fixed in the memory of Almighty God.

One can rob a neighbor of possessions, opportunity, or freedom. One can weave an insidious web of lies to convince

others that certain groups are unde-
serving of respect. Yet, try as one
might, one can never take away the
name of a fellow human being.

Sacred Scripture teaches us the
importance of names in conferring
upon someone a unique mission or
a special gift. God called Abram
"Abraham" because he was to
become the "father of many nations"
(Gen 17:5). Jacob was called
"Israel" because he had "contended
with God and man and prevailed"
(Gen 32:29). The names enshrined
in this hallowed monument will
forever hold a sacred place among

Ronen Zvulun/REUTERS

Pope Benedict XVI observes
a moment of silence during
the ceremony in the
Hall of Remembrance at
Yad Vashem Holocaust
Memorial in Jerusalem.

the countless descendants of Abraham. Like his, their faith
was tested. Like Jacob, they were immersed in the struggle to
discern the designs of the Almighty. May the names of these
victims never perish! May their suffering never be denied,
belittled, or forgotten! And may all people of goodwill
remain vigilant in rooting out from the heart of man any-
thing that could lead to tragedies such as this!

The Catholic Church, committed to the teachings of
Jesus and intent on imitating his love for all people, feels
deep compassion for the victims remembered here. Similarly,
she draws close to all those who today are subjected to
persecution on account of race, color, condition of life, or
religion—their sufferings are hers, and hers is their hope for
justice. As Bishop of Rome and Successor of the Apostle
Peter, I reaffirm—like my predecessors—that the Church is
committed to praying and working tirelessly to ensure that
hatred will never reign in the hearts of men again. The

Ronen Zvulun/REUTERS

Rabbi Israel Meir Lau greets Pope Benedict XVI in the Hall of Remembrance at Yad Vashem Holocaust Memorial in Jerusalem.

God of Abraham, Isaac, and Jacob is the God of peace (cf. Ps 85:9).

The Scriptures teach that it is our task to remind the world that this God lives, even though we sometimes find it difficult to grasp his mysterious and inscrutable ways. He has revealed himself and continues to work in human history. He alone governs the world with righteousness and judges all peoples with fairness (cf. Ps 9:9).

Gazing upon the faces reflected in the pool that lies in stillness within this memorial, one cannot help but recall how each of them bears a name. I can only imagine the joyful expectation of their parents as they anxiously awaited the birth of their children. What name shall we give this child? What is to become of him or her? Who could have imagined that they would be condemned to such a deplorable fate!

As we stand here in silence, their cry still echoes in our hearts. It is a cry raised against every act of injustice and violence. It is a perpetual reproach against the spilling of innocent blood. It is the cry of Abel rising from the earth to the

Ronen Zvulun/REUTERS

Pope Benedict XVI greets Holocaust survivors in the
Hall of Remembrance at Yad Vashem Holocaust Memorial in Jerusalem.

Almighty. Professing our steadfast trust in God, we give voice to that cry using words from the Book of Lamentations which are full of significance for both Jews and Christians:

"The favors of the Lord are not exhausted,
his mercies are not spent;
They are renewed each morning,
so great is his faithfulness.
"My portion is the Lord," says my soul;
"therefore will I hope in him."

Good is the Lord to the one who waits for him,
to the soul that seeks him;
It is good to hope in silence
for the saving help of the Lord." (Lam 3:22–26)

My dear friends, I am deeply grateful to God and to you for the opportunity to stand here in silence: a silence to remember, a silence to pray, a silence to hope.

SIGNATURE OF THE HOLY FATHER

Monday, 11 May 2009

"His mercies are not spent."

The Book of Lamentations 3:22

Benedictus PP. XVI.

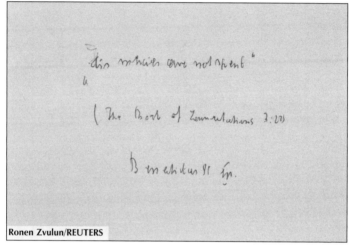

Ronen Zvulun/REUTERS

A note written by Pope Benedict XVI during his visit at Yad Vashem Holocaust Memorial in Jerusalem is seen in their guestbook.

Day Four: May 11, 2009

15

MEETING WITH ORGANIZATIONS FOR INTERRELIGIOUS DIALOGUE

Auditorium of Notre Dame Center, Jerusalem

Dear Brother Bishops,
Distinguished Religious Leaders,
Dear Friends,

It is a source of great joy for me to meet with you this evening. I wish to thank His Beatitude Patriarch Fouad Twal for his kind words of welcome spoken on behalf of everyone present. I reciprocate the warm sentiments expressed and gladly greet all of you and the members of the groups and organizations you represent.

"God said to Abram, 'Go from your country, your kindred and your father's house for a land I shall show you'...so Abram went...and took his wife Sarah with him" (Gen 12:1–5). God's irruptive call, which marks the beginning of the history of our faith traditions, was heard in the midst of man's ordinary daily existence. And the history that ensued was shaped, not in isolation, but through the encounter with Egyptian, Hittite, Sumerian, Babylonian, Persian, and Greek cultures.

Faith is always lived within a culture. The history of religion shows that a community of believers proceeds by degrees of faithfulness to God, drawing from and shaping

— 65 —

the culture it meets. This same dynamic is found in individual believers from the great monotheistic traditions: attuned to the voice of God, like Abraham we respond to his call and set out seeking the fulfillment of his promises, striving to obey his will, forging a path in our own particular culture.

Today, nearly four thousand years after Abraham, the encounter of religions with culture occurs not simply on a geographical plane. Certain aspects of globalization, and in particular the world of the Internet, have created a vast virtual culture, the worth of which is as varied as its countless manifestations. Undoubtedly much has been achieved to create a sense of closeness and unity within the worldwide human family. Yet, at the same time, the boundless array of portals through which people so readily access undifferentiated sources of information can easily become an instrument of increasing fragmentation: the unity of knowledge is shattered and the complex skills of critique, discernment, and discrimination learned through academic and ethical traditions are at times bypassed or neglected.

The question naturally arises then as to what contribution religion makes to the cultures of the world against the backdrop of rapid globalization. Since many are quick to point out the readily apparent differences between religions, as believers or religious persons we are presented with the challenge to proclaim with clarity what we share in common.

Abraham's first step in faith—and our steps to or from the synagogue, church, mosque or temple—tread the path of our single human history, unfolding along the way, we might say, to the eternal Jerusalem (cf. Rev 21:23). Similarly, every culture with its inner capacity to give and receive gives expression to the one human nature. Yet, the individual is never fully expressed through his or her own culture, but transcends it in the constant search for something beyond.

From this perspective, dear friends, we see the possibility of a unity that is not dependent upon uniformity. While the differences we explore in interreligious dialogue may at times appear as barriers, they need not overshadow the common sense of awe and respect for the universal, for the absolute, and for truth, which impel religious peoples to converse with one another in the first place. Indeed, it is the shared conviction that these transcendent realities have their source in—and bear traces of—the Almighty that believers uphold before each other, our organizations, our society, our world. In this way not only do we enrich culture but we shape it: lives of religious fidelity echo God's irruptive presence and so form a culture not defined by boundaries of time or place but fundamentally shaped by the principles and actions that stem from belief.

Religious belief presupposes truth. The one who believes is the one who seeks truth and lives by it. Although the medium by which we understand the discovery and communication of truth differs in part from religion to religion, we should not be deterred in our efforts to bear witness to truth's power. Together we can proclaim that God exists and can be known, that the earth is his creation, that we are his creatures, and that he calls every man and woman to a way of life that respects his design for the world. Friends, if we believe we have a criterion of judgment and discernment that is divine in origin and intended for all humanity, then we cannot tire of bringing that knowledge to bear on civic life. Truth should be offered to all; it serves all members of society. It sheds light on the foundation of morality and ethics, and suffuses reason with the strength to reach beyond its own limitations in order to give expression to our deepest common aspirations. Far from threatening the tolerance of differences or cultural plurality, truth makes consensus possible, keeps public debate rational, honest, and accountable, and opens the gateway to peace. Fostering the will to be obedient to the truth in fact broadens our concept of reason and its scope of application and makes possible the genuine dialogue of cultures and religions so urgently needed today.

Each one of us here also knows, however, that God's voice is heard less-clearly today, and reason itself has in so many instances become deaf to the divine. Yet that "void" is not one of silence. Indeed, it is the din of egotistical demands, empty promises, and false hopes that so often invades the very space in which God seeks us. Can we then make spaces—oases of peace and profound reflection— where God's voice can be heard anew; where his truth can be discovered within the universality of reason; where every individual, regardless of dwelling, or ethnic group, or political hue, or religious belief, can be respected as a person, as a fellow human being? In an age of instant access to information and social tendencies that engender a kind of monoculture, deep reflection against the backdrop of God's presence will embolden reason, stimulate creative genius, facilitate critical appreciation of cultural practices, and uphold the universal value of religious belief.

Friends, the institutions and groups that you represent engage in interreligious dialogue and the promotion of cultural initiatives at a wide range of levels. From academic institutions—and here I wish to make special mention of the outstanding achievements of Bethlehem University—to bereaved parents groups, from initiatives through music and the arts to the courageous example of ordinary mothers and fathers, from formal dialogue groups to charitable organizations, you daily demonstrate your belief that our duty before God is expressed not only in our worship but also in our love and concern for society, for culture, for our world, and for all who live in this land. Some would have us believe that our differences are necessarily a cause of division and thus at most to be tolerated. A few even maintain that our voices should simply be silenced. But we know that our differences need never be misrepresented as an inevitable source of friction or tension either between ourselves or within society at large. Rather, they provide a wonderful opportunity for people of different religions to live together in profound respect, esteem, and appreciation, encouraging one another in the ways of God. Prompted by the Almighty and enlightened by his truth, may you continue to step forward with courage, respecting all that differentiates us and promoting all that unites us as creatures blessed with the desire to bring hope to our communities and world. May God guide us along this path!

Day Five

May 12, 2009

16

COURTESY VISIT TO THE GRAND MUFTI OF JERUSALEM AT THE MOUNT OF THE TEMPLE

Dear Muslim Friends,
As-salámu 'aláikum! Peace upon you!

I cordially thank the Grand Mufti, Muhammad Ahmad Hussein, together with the director of the Jerusalem Islamic Waqf, Sheikh Mohammed Azzam al-Khatib al-Tamimi, and the head of the Awquaf Council, Sheikh Abdel Azim Salhab, for the welcome they have extended to me on your behalf. I am deeply grateful for the invitation to visit this sacred place, and I willingly pay my respects to you and the leaders of the Islamic community in Jerusalem.

The Dome of the Rock draws our hearts and minds to reflect upon the mystery of creation and the faith of Abraham. Here the paths of the world's three great monotheistic religions meet, reminding us what they share in common. Each believes in One God, creator and ruler of all. Each recognizes Abraham as a forefather, a man of faith upon whom God bestowed a special blessing. Each has gained a large following throughout the centuries and inspired a rich spiritual, intellectual, and cultural patrimony.

In a world sadly torn by divisions, this sacred place serves as a stimulus, and also challenges men and women of goodwill, to work to overcome misunderstandings and con-

REUTERS/L'Osservatore Romano

Pope Benedict XVI walks in front of the Dome of the Rock, on the compound known to Muslims as al-Haram al-Sharif (Noble Sanctuary) and to Jews as Temple Mount, in Jerusalem's Old City.

flicts of the past and to set out on the path of a sincere dialogue aimed at building a world of justice and peace for coming generations.

Since the teachings of religious traditions ultimately concern the reality of God, the meaning of life, and the common destiny of mankind—that is to say, all that is most sacred and dear to us—there may be a temptation to engage in such dialogue with reluctance or ambivalence about its possibilities for success. Yet we can begin with the belief that the One God is the infinite source of justice and mercy, since in him the two exist in perfect unity. Those who confess his name are entrusted with the task of striving tirelessly for righteousness while imitating his forgiveness, for both are intrinsically oriented to the peaceful and harmonious coexistence of the human family.

For this reason, it is paramount that those who adore the One God should show themselves to be both grounded in and directed toward the unity of the entire human family. In other words, fidelity to the One God, the Creator, the

Most High, leads to the recognition that human beings are fundamentally interrelated, since all owe their very existence to a single source and are pointed toward a common goal. Imprinted with the indelible image of the divine, they are called to play an active role in mending divisions and promoting human solidarity.

This places a grave responsibility upon us. Those who honor the One God believe that he will hold human beings accountable for their actions. Christians assert that the divine gifts of reason and freedom stand at the basis of this accountability. Reason opens the mind to grasp the shared nature and common destiny of the human family, while freedom moves the heart to accept the other and serve him in charity. Undivided love for the One God and charity toward one's neighbor thus become the fulcrum around which all else turns. This is why we work untiringly to safeguard human hearts from hatred, anger, or vengeance.

Dear friends, I have come to Jerusalem on a journey of faith. I thank God for this occasion to meet you as the Bishop of Rome and Successor of the Apostle Peter, but also as a child of Abraham, by whom "all the families of the earth find blessing" (Gen 12:3; cf. Rom 4:16–17). I assure you of the Church's ardent desire to cooperate for the well-being of the human family. She firmly believes that the fulfillment of the promise made to Abraham is universal in scope, embracing all men and women regardless of provenance or social status. As Muslims and Christians further the respectful dialogue they have already begun, I pray that they will explore how the Oneness of God is inextricably tied to the unity of the human family. In submitting to his loving plan for creation, in studying the law inscribed in the cosmos and implanted in the human heart, in reflecting upon the mysterious gift of God's self-revelation, may all his followers continue to keep their gaze fixed on his absolute goodness, never losing sight of the way it is reflected in the faces of others.

With these thoughts, I humbly ask the Almighty to grant you peace and to bless all the beloved people of this region. May we strive to live in a spirit of harmony and cooperation, bearing witness to the One God by generously serving one another. Thank you!

17

PRAYER AT THE WESTERN WALL

God of all the ages,
on my visit to Jerusalem, the "City of Peace,"
spiritual home to Jews, Christians and Muslims alike,
I bring before you the joys, the hopes, and the aspirations,
the trials, the suffering, and the pain, of all your people
throughout the world.

Pierpaolo Cito/REUTERS

Pope Benedict XVI, flanked by his assistant Monsignor Guido Marini,
puts a note in the Western Wall, Judaism's holiest prayer site,
in Jerusalem's Old City.

God of Abraham, Isaac, and Jacob,
hear the cry of the afflicted, the fearful, the bereft;
send your peace upon this Holy Land, upon the Middle
    East,
upon the entire human family;
stir the hearts of all who call upon your name,
to walk humbly in the path of justice and compassion.

"The Lord is good to those who wait for him,
to the soul that seeks him!" (Lam 3:25)

18

COURTESY VISIT TO THE TWO CHIEF RABBIS OF JERUSALEM AT THE HECHAL SHLOMO CENTER

Distinguished Rabbis,
Dear Friends,

    I am grateful for the invitation to visit Hechal Shlomo and to meet with you during this trip of mine to the Holy Land as Bishop of Rome. I thank Sephardi Rabbi Shlomo Amar and Ashkenazi Rabbi Yona Metzger for their warm words of welcome and the desire they have expressed to continue strengthening the bonds of friendship that the Catholic Church and the Chief Rabbinate have labored so diligently to forge over the past decades. Your visits to the Vatican in 2003 and 2005 are a sign of the goodwill that characterizes our developing relations.

    Distinguished rabbis, I reciprocate by expressing my own respect and esteem for you and your communities. I assure you of my desire to deepen mutual understanding and cooperation between the Holy See, the Chief Rabbinate of Israel, and Jewish people throughout the world.

A great source of satisfaction for me since the beginning of my pontificate has been the fruit yielded by the ongoing dialogue between the Delegation of the Holy See's Commission for Religious Relations with the Jews and the Chief Rabbinate of Israel's Delegation for Relations with the Catholic Church. I wish to thank the members of both delegations for their dedication and hard work in implementing this initiative, so earnestly desired by my esteemed predecessor Pope John Paul II, as he said during the Great Jubilee Year of 2000.

Our encounter today is a most fitting occasion to give thanks to the Almighty for the many blessings that have accompanied the dialogue conducted by the bilateral commission, and to look forward with expectation to its future sessions. The willingness of the delegates to discuss openly and patiently not only points of agreement, but also points of difference, has already paved the way to more effective collaboration in public life. Jews and Christians alike are concerned to ensure respect for the sacredness of human life, the centrality of the family, a sound education for the young, and the freedom of religion and conscience for a healthy society. These themes of dialogue represent only the initial phases of what we trust will be a steady, progressive journey toward an enhanced mutual understanding.

An indication of the potential of this series of meetings is readily seen in our shared concern in the face of moral relativism and the offences it spawns against the dignity of the human person. In approaching the most urgent ethical questions of our day, our two communities are challenged to engage people of goodwill at the level of reason, while simultaneously pointing to the religious foundations that best sus-

Kobi Gideon /REUTERS

Pope Benedict receives a gift during a meeting with Israel's Chief Sephardic Rabbi Shlomo Ammar (r.) and Chief Ashkenazi Rabbi Yona Metzger (l.) at the Jewish Heritage Center in Jerusalem.

tain lasting moral values. May the dialogue that has begun continue to generate ideas on how Christians and Jews can work together to heighten society's appreciation of the distinctive contribution of our religious and ethical traditions. Here in Israel, given that Christians constitute only a small portion of the total population, they particularly value opportunities for dialogue with their Jewish neighbors.

Trust is undeniably an essential element of effective dialogue. Today I have the opportunity to repeat that the Catholic Church is irrevocably committed to the path chosen at the Second Vatican Council for a genuine and lasting reconciliation between Christians and Jews. As the declaration *Nostra Aetate* makes clear, the Church continues to value the spiritual patrimony common to Christians and Jews and desires an ever-deeper, mutual understanding and respect through biblical and theological studies, as well as fraternal dialogues. May the seven bilateral commission meetings that have already taken place between the Holy See and the Chief Rabbinate stand as evidence! I am thus grateful for your reciprocal assurance that the relationship between the Catholic Church and the Chief Rabbinate will continue to grow in respect and understanding in the future.

My friends, I express again my deep appreciation for the welcome you have extended to me today. I am confident that our friendship will continue to set an example of trust in dialogue for Jews and Christians throughout the world. Looking at the accomplishments achieved thus far, and drawing our inspiration from the Holy Scriptures, we can confidently look forward to even stronger cooperation between our communities—together with all people of goodwill—in decrying hatred and oppression throughout the world. I pray that God, who searches our hearts and knows our thoughts (Ps 139:23), will continue to enlighten us with his wisdom, so that we may follow his commandments to love him with all our heart, soul, and strength (cf. Deut 6:5), and to love our neighbor as ourselves (Lev 19:18). Thank you.

19

REGINA COELI PRAYER WITH THE ORDINARIES OF THE HOLY LAND IN THE UPPER ROOM, JERUSALEM

Dear Brother Bishops,
Dear Father Custos,

It is with great joy that I greet you, the ordinaries of the Holy Land, in this Upper Room, where, according to tradition, the Lord opened his heart to his chosen disciples and celebrated the Paschal Mystery, and where the Holy Spirit on the day of Pentecost inspired the early disciples to go forth and preach the good news. I thank Father Pizzaballa for the warm words of welcome which he has expressed to me on your behalf. You represent the Catholic communities of the Holy Land that, in their faith and devotion, are like lighted candles illuminating the holy places that were graced by the presence of Jesus our living Lord. This unique privilege gives you and your people a special place of affection in my heart as the Successor of Peter.

"When Jesus knew that his hour had come to depart from this world to the Father, having loved his own who were in the world, he loved them to the end" (John 13:1). The Upper Room recalls the last supper of our Lord with Peter and the other apostles and invites the Church to prayerful contemplation. In this vein, we gather together, the Successor of Peter with successors of the apostles, in this same place where Jesus revealed in the offering of his own body and blood, the new depths of the covenant of love established between God and his people. In the Upper Room, the mystery of grace and salvation, of which we are recipients and also heralds and ministers, can be expressed only in terms of love. Because he has loved us first and continues to do so, we can respond with love (cf. *Deus Caritas Est*, 2). Our life as Christians is not simply a human effort to live the demands of the Gospel imposed upon us as duties. In the Eucharist, we are drawn into the mystery of divine love. Our lives become a grateful, docile, and active acceptance of the power of a love that is given to us. This transforming love, which is grace and truth (cf. John 1:17), prompts us, as individuals and communities, to overcome the temptation to turn in upon ourselves in selfishness, indolence, isolation, prejudice, or fear, and to give ourselves generously to the Lord and to others. It moves us as Christian communities to be faithful to our mission with frankness and courage (cf. Acts 4:13). In the Good Shepherd who lays down his life for his flock, in the Teacher who washes the feet of his disciples, you find, my dear brothers, the model of your own ministry in the service of our God who promotes love and communion.

The call to communion of mind and heart, so closely related to the commandment of love and to the central unifying role of the Eucharist in our lives, is of special relevance in the Holy Land. The different Christian Churches found here represent a rich and varied spiritual patrimony and are a sign of the multiple forms of interaction between the Gospel and different cultures. They also remind us that the mission of the Church is to preach the universal love of God and to gather, from far and near, all who are called by him, in such a way that, with their traditions and their talents, they form the one family of God. A new spiritual impulse toward communion in diversity within the Catholic Church and a new ecumenical awareness have marked our times, especially since the Second Vatican Council. The Spirit moves our hearts gently toward humility and peace, toward mutual acceptance, comprehension, and cooperation. This inner disposition to unity under the prompting of the Holy Spirit is decisive if Christians are to fulfill their mission in the world (cf. John 17:21).

In the measure in which the gift of love is accepted and grows in the Church, the Christian presence in the Holy Land and in the neighboring regions will be vibrant. This presence is of vital importance for the good of society as a whole. The clear words of Jesus on the intimate bond between love of God and love of neighbor, on mercy and compassion, on meekness, peace, and forgiveness, are a leaven capable of transforming hearts and shaping actions. Christians in the Middle East, together with other people of goodwill, are contributing, as loyal and responsible citizens, in spite of difficulties and restrictions, to the promotion and consolidation of a climate of peace in diversity. I wish to repeat to them what I stated in my 2006 Christmas message to Catholics in the Middle East: "I express with affection my personal closeness in this situation of human insecurity, daily suffering, fear, and hope that you are living. I repeat to your communities the words of the Redeemer: 'Fear not little flock, for it is your Father's good pleasure to give you the Kingdom'" (Luke 12:32; Christmas Message to Catholics living in the Middle East Region, 21 December 2006).

Dear brother bishops, count on my support and encouragement as you do all that is in your power to assist our Christian brothers and sisters to remain and prosper here in the land of their ancestors and to be messengers and promoters of peace. I appreciate your efforts to offer them, as mature and responsible citizens, spiritual sustenance, values, and principles that assist them in playing their role in society. Through education, professional preparation, and other social and economic initiatives, their condition will be sustained and improved. For my part, I renew my appeal to our brothers and sisters worldwide to support and to remember in their prayers the Christian communities of the Holy Land and the Middle East. In this context, I wish to express my appreciation for the service offered to the many pilgrims and visitors who come to the Holy Land seeking inspiration and renewal in the footsteps of Jesus. The Gospel story, contemplated in its historical and geographical setting, becomes vivid and colorful; a clearer grasp of the significance of the Lord's words and deeds is obtained. Many memorable experiences of pilgrims to the Holy Land have been possible, thanks also to the hospitality and fraternal guidance offered by you, especially by the Franciscan Friars of the Custody. For this service, I wish to assure you of the appreciation and gratitude of the Universal Church, and I express the wish that many more pilgrims will visit in the future.

Dear brothers, as we address together our joyful prayer to Mary, Queen of Heaven, let us place confidently in her hands the well-being and spiritual renewal of all Christians in the Holy Land, so that, under the guidance of their pastors, they may grow in faith, hope, and love, and persevere in their mission as promoters of communion and peace.

20

VISIT TO THE CO-CATHEDRAL OF THE LATINS

Your Beatitude,

I thank you for your words of welcome. I also greet the Patriarch Emeritus and I assure you both of my fraternal good wishes and prayers.

Dear brothers and sisters in Christ, I am happy to be here with you today in this Co-Cathedral, where the Christian community in Jerusalem continues to gather, as it has been doing for centuries, ever since the earliest days of the Church. Here in this city, Peter first preached the good news of Jesus Christ on the day of Pentecost, when about three thousand souls were added to the number of the disciples. Here too is where the first Christians "devoted themselves to the apostles' teaching and fellowship, to the breaking of bread and the prayers" (Acts 2:42). From Jerusalem, the Gospel has gone out "to all the earth...to the ends of the

world" (Ps 19:4); all the time, the Church's missionary effort
has been sustained by the prayers of the faithful, gathered
around the altar of the Lord, invoking the mighty power of
the Holy Spirit upon the work of preaching.

Above all, it is the prayers of those whose vocation, in
the words of Saint Thérèse of Lisieux, is to be "love, deep
down in the heart of the Church" (Letter to Sister Marie of
the Sacred Heart) that sustains the work of evangelization. I
want to express a particular word of appreciation for the
hidden apostolate of the contemplatives who are present
here, and to thank you for your generous dedication to lives
of prayer and self-denial. I am especially grateful for the
prayers you offer for my universal ministry, and I ask you to
continue to commend to the Lord my work of service to
God's people all over the world. In the words of the Psalmist,
I ask you also to "pray for the peace of Jerusalem" (Ps
122:6), to pray without ceasing for an end to the conflict
that has brought so much suffering to the peoples of this
land. And now, I give you my blessing.

21

HOMILY AT MASS CELEBRATED IN THE VALLEY OF JOSAPHAT, JERUSALEM

Dear Brothers and Sisters in the Lord,

"Christ is risen, alleluia!" With these words I greet you
with immense affection. I thank Patriarch Fouad Twal for
his words of welcome on your behalf, and before all else, I
express my joy at being able to celebrate this Eucharist with

you, the Church in Jerusalem. We are gathered beneath the Mount of Olives, where our Lord prayed and suffered, where he wept for love of this city and the desire that it should know "the path to peace" (Luke 19:42), and whence he returned to the Father, giving his final earthly blessing to his disciples and to us. Today let us accept this blessing. He gives it in a special way to you, dear brothers and sisters, who stand in an unbroken line with those first disciples who encountered the Risen Lord in the breaking of the bread, those who experienced the outpouring of the Spirit in the Upper Room and those who were converted by the preaching of Saint Peter and the other apostles. My greeting also goes to all those present, and in a special way to those faithful of the Holy Land who for various reasons were not able to be with us today.

As the Successor of Saint Peter, I have retraced his steps in order to proclaim the Risen Christ in your midst, to confirm you in the faith of your fathers, and to invoke upon you the consolation which is the gift of the Paraclete. Standing before you today, I wish to acknowledge the difficulties, the frustration, and the pain and suffering that so many of you have endured as a result of the conflicts that have afflicted these lands, and the bitter experiences of displacement that so many of your families have known and—God forbid—may yet know. I hope my presence here is a sign that you are not forgotten, that your persevering presence and witness are indeed precious in God's eyes and integral to the future of these lands. Precisely because of your deep roots in this land, your ancient and strong Christian culture, and your unwavering trust in God's promises, you, the Christians of the Holy Land, are called to serve not only as a beacon of faith to the universal Church, but also as a leaven of harmony, wisdom, and equilibrium in the life of a society that has traditionally been, and continues to be, pluralistic, multiethnic, and multireligious.

In today's second reading, the Apostle Paul tells the Colossians to "seek the things that are above, where Christ is seated at the right hand of God" (Col 3:1). His words resound with particular force here, beneath the Garden of Gethsemane, where Jesus accepted the chalice of suffering in complete obedience to the Father's will and where, according to tradition, he ascended to the right hand of the Father to make perpetual intercession for us, the members of his Body. Saint Paul, the great herald of Christian hope, knew the cost of that hope, its price in suffering and persecution for the sake of the Gospel, yet he never wavered in his conviction that Christ's resurrection was the beginning of a new creation. As he tells us: "When Christ, who is your life, is revealed, you too will be revealed with him in glory!" (Col 3:4).

Paul's exhortation to "set our minds on the things that are above" must constantly echo in our hearts. His words point us to the fulfillment of faith's vision in that heavenly Jerusalem where, in fidelity to the ancient prophecies, God will wipe away the tears from every eye, and prepare a banquet of salvation for all peoples (cf. Isa 25:6–8; Rev 21:2–4).

This is the hope, this the vision, that inspires all who love this earthly Jerusalem to see her as a prophecy and promise of that universal reconciliation and peace that God desires for the whole human family. Sadly, beneath the walls of this same city, we are also led to consider how far our world is from the complete fulfillment of that prophecy and promise. In this Holy City where life conquered death, where the Spirit was poured out as the first-fruits of the new creation, hope continues to battle despair, frustration, and cynicism, while the peace that is God's gift and call continues to be threatened by selfishness, conflict, division, and the burden of past wrongs. For this reason, the Christian community in this city that beheld the resurrection of Christ and the outpouring of the Spirit must hold fast all the more to the hope bestowed by the Gospel, cherishing the pledge of Christ's definitive victory over sin and death, bearing witness to the power of forgiveness, and showing forth the Church's deepest nature as the sign and sacrament of a humanity reconciled, renewed, and made one in Christ, the new Adam.

Gathered beneath the walls of this city, sacred to the followers of three great religions, how can we not turn our thoughts to Jerusalem's universal vocation? Heralded by the prophets, this vocation also emerges as an indisputable fact, a reality irrevocably grounded in the complex history of this city and its people. Jews, Muslims, and Christians alike call this city their spiritual home. How much needs to be done to make it truly a "city of peace" for all peoples, where all can come in pilgrimage in search of God, and hear his voice, "a voice which speaks of peace!" (cf. Ps 85:8)

Jerusalem, in fact, has always been a city whose streets echo with different languages, whose stones are trod by people of every race and tongue, whose walls are a symbol of God's provident care for the whole human family. As a microcosm of our globalized world, this city, if it is to live up to its universal vocation, must be a place that teaches universality, respect for others, dialogue, and mutual understanding; a place where prejudice, ignorance, and the fear that fuels them, are overcome by honesty, integrity, and the pursuit of peace. There should be no place within these walls for narrowness, discrimination, violence, and injustice. Believers in a God of mercy—whether they identify themselves as Jews, Christians, or Muslims—must be the first to promote this culture of reconciliation and peace, however painstakingly slow the process may be, and however burdensome the weight of past memories.

Here I would like to speak directly to the tragic reality—which cannot fail to be a source of concern to all who love this city and this land—of the departure of so many members of the Christian community in recent years. While understandable reasons lead many, especially the young, to emigrate, this decision brings in its wake a great cultural and spiritual impoverishment to the city. Today I wish to repeat what I have said on other occasions: in the Holy Land there is room for everyone! As I urge the authorities to respect, to support, and to value the Christian presence here, I also wish to assure you of the solidarity, love, and support of the whole Church and of the Holy See.

Dear friends, in the Gospel we have just heard, Saint Peter and Saint John run to the empty tomb, and John, we are told, "saw and believed" (John 20:8). Here in the Holy Land, with the eyes of faith, you, together with the pilgrims from throughout the world who throng its churches and shrines, are blessed to "see" the places hallowed by Christ's presence, his earthly ministry, his passion, death, and resurrection, and the gift of his Holy Spirit. Here, like the Apostle Saint Thomas, you are granted the opportunity to "touch" the historical realities that underlie our confession of faith in the Son of God. My prayer for you today is that you continue, day by day, to "see and believe" in the signs of God's providence and unfailing mercy, to "hear" with renewed faith and hope the consoling words of the apostolic preaching, to "touch" the sources of grace in the sacraments, and to incarnate for others their pledge of new beginnings, the freedom born of forgiveness, the interior light and peace that can bring healing and hope to even the darkest of human realities.

In the Church of the Holy Sepulcher, pilgrims in every century have venerated the stone that tradition tells us stood before the entrance to the tomb on the morning of Christ's resurrection. Let us return frequently to that empty tomb. There let us reaffirm our faith in the victory of life, and pray that every "heavy stone" that stands before the door of our hearts, blocking our complete surrender to the Lord in faith, hope, and love, may be shattered by the power of the light and life that shone forth from Jerusalem to all the world that first Easter morn. Christ is risen, alleluia! He is truly risen, alleluia!

Day Six

May 13, 2009

22

WELCOMING CEREMONY IN THE SQUARE IN FRONT OF THE PRESIDENTIAL PALACE, BETHLEHEM

Mr. President,
Dear Friends,

I greet all of you from my heart, and I warmly thank the president, Mr. Mahmoud Abbas, for his words of welcome. My pilgrimage to the lands of the Bible would not be complete without a visit to Bethlehem, the City of David and the birthplace of Jesus Christ. Nor could I come to the Holy Land without accepting the kind invitation of President Abbas to visit these Territories and to greet the Palestinian people. I know how much you have suffered and continue to suffer as a result of the turmoil that has afflicted this land for decades. My heart goes out to all the families who have been left homeless. This afternoon I will pay a visit to the Aida Refugee Camp in order to express my solidarity with the people who have lost so much. To those among you who mourn the loss of family members and loved ones in the hostilities, particularly the recent conflict in Gaza, I offer an assurance of deep compassion and frequent remembrance in prayer. Indeed, I keep all of you in my daily prayers, and I earnestly beg the

Almighty for peace, a just and lasting peace, in the Palestinian Territories and throughout the region.

Mr. President, the Holy See supports the right of your people to a sovereign Palestinian homeland in the land of your forefathers, secure and at peace with its neighbors, within internationally recognized borders. Even if at present that goal seems far from being realized, I urge you and all your people to keep alive the flame of hope, hope that a way can be found of meeting the legitimate aspirations of both Israelis and Palestinians for peace and stability. In the words of the late Pope John Paul II, there can be "no peace without justice, no justice without forgiveness" (Message for the 2002 World Day of Peace). I plead with all the parties to this long-standing conflict to put aside whatever grievances and divisions still stand in the way of reconciliation, and to reach out with generosity and compassion to all alike, without discrimination. Just and peaceful coexistence among the peoples of the Middle East can only be achieved through a spirit of cooperation and mutual respect, in which the rights and dignity of all are acknowledged and upheld. I ask all of you, I ask your leaders, to make a renewed commitment to work toward these goals. In particular I call on the international community to bring its influence to bear in favor of a solution. Believe and trust that through honest and persevering dialogue, with full respect for the demands of justice, lasting peace really can be attained in these lands.

It is my earnest hope that the serious concerns involving security in Israel and the Palestinian Territories will soon be allayed sufficiently to allow greater freedom of movement, especially with regard to contact between family members and access to the holy places. Palestinians, like any other people, have a natural right to marry, to raise families, and to have access to work, education, and health care. I pray too that, with the assistance of the international community, reconstruction work can proceed swiftly wherever homes, schools, or hospitals have been damaged or destroyed, especially during the recent fighting in Gaza. This is essential if the people of this land are to live in conditions conducive to lasting peace and prosperity. A stable infrastructure will provide your young people with better opportunities to acquire valuable skills and to seek gainful employment, enabling them to play their part in building up the life of your communities. I make this appeal to the many young people throughout the Palestinian Territories today: do not allow the loss of life and the destruction that you have witnessed to arouse bitterness or resentment in your hearts. Have the courage to resist any temptation you may feel to resort to acts of violence or terrorism. Instead, let what you have experienced renew your determination to build peace. Let it fill you with a deep desire to make a lasting contribution to the future of Palestine, so that it can take its rightful place on the world stage. Let it inspire in you sentiments of compassion for all who suffer, zeal for reconciliation, and a firm belief in the possibility of a brighter future.

Mr. President, dear friends gathered here in Bethlehem, I invoke upon all the Palestinian people the blessings and the protection of our heavenly Father, and I pray fervently that the song that the angels sang here in this place will be fulfilled: peace on earth, goodwill among men. Thank you. And may God be with you.

23

HOMILY AT MASS CELEBRATED IN MANGER SQUARE, BETHLEHEM

Dear Brothers and Sisters in Christ,

I thank Almighty God for giving me the grace to come to Bethlehem, not only to venerate the place of Christ's birth, but also to stand beside you, my brothers and sisters in the faith, in these Palestinian Territories. I am grateful to Patriarch Fouad Twal for the sentiments that he has expressed on your behalf, and I greet with affection my brother bishops and all the priests, religious, and lay faithful who labor daily to confirm this local Church in faith, hope, and love. In a special way my heart goes out to the pilgrims from war-torn Gaza: I ask you to bring back to your families and your communities my warm embrace, and my sorrow for the loss, the hardship, and the suffering you have had to endure. Please be assured of my solidarity with you in the immense work of rebuilding that now lies ahead, and my prayers that the embargo will soon be lifted.

"Do not be afraid; for behold I proclaim to you good news of great joy....Today in the city of David a Savior is born for you" (Luke 2:10–11). The message of Christ's coming, brought from heaven by the voice of angels, continues to echo in this town, just as it echoes in families, homes, and communities throughout the world. It is "good news," the angels say, "for all the people." It proclaims that the Messiah— the Son of God and the Son of David—has been born "for you": for you and me, and for men and women in every time and place. In God's plan, Bethlehem, "least among the clans of Judah" (Mic 5:2), has become a place of undying glory: the place where, in the fullness of time, God chose to become man, to end the long reign of sin and death, and to bring new and abundant life to a world that had grown old, weary, and oppressed by hopelessness.

For men and women everywhere, Bethlehem is associated with this joyful message of rebirth, renewal, light, and freedom. Yet here, in our midst, how far this magnificent promise seems from being realized! How distant seems that Kingdom of wide dominion and peace, security, justice, and integrity that the prophet Isaiah heralded in the first reading (cf. Isa 9:7), and that we proclaim as definitively established in the coming of Jesus Christ, Messiah, and King!

From the day of his birth, Jesus was "a sign of contradiction" (Luke 2:34), and he continues to be so, even today. The Lord of hosts, "whose origin is from old, from ancient days" (Mic 5:2), wished to inaugurate his Kingdom by being born in this little town, entering our world in the silence and humility of a cave and lying, a helpless babe, in a manger. Here, in Bethlehem, amid every kind of contradiction, the stones continue to cry out this "good news," the message of redemption that this city, above all others, is called to proclaim to the world. For here, in a way that surpassed every human hope and expectation, God proved faithful to his promises. In the birth of his Son, he revealed the coming of a Kingdom of love: a divine love that stoops down in order to bring healing and lift us up; a love that is revealed in the humiliation and weakness of the Cross, yet triumphs in a glorious resurrection to new life. Christ brought a Kingdom that is not of this world, yet a Kingdom that is capable of changing this world, for it has the power to change hearts, to enlighten minds, and to strengthen wills. By taking on our flesh, with all its weaknesses, and transfiguring it by the power of his Spirit, Jesus has called us to be witnesses of his victory over sin and death. And this is what the message of Bethlehem calls us to be: witnesses of the triumph of God's love over the hatred, selfishness, fear, and resentment that cripple human relationships and create division where brothers should dwell in unity, destruction where men should be building, and despair where hope should flourish!

"In hope we were saved," the Apostle Paul says (Rom 8:24). Yet he affirms with utter realism that creation continues to groan in travail, even as we, who have received the first-fruits of the Spirit, patiently await the fulfillment of our redemption (cf. Rom 8:22–24). In today's second reading, Paul draws a lesson from the Incarnation that is particularly applicable to the travail which you, God's chosen ones in Bethlehem, are experiencing: "God's grace has appeared," he tells us, "training us to reject godless ways and worldly desires, and to live, temperately, justly, and devoutly in this age," as we await the coming of our blessed hope, the Savior Jesus Christ (Titus 2:11–13).

Are these not the virtues required of men and women who live in hope? First, the constant conversion to Christ, which is reflected not only in our actions but also in our reasoning: the courage to abandon fruitless and sterile ways of thinking, acting, and reacting. Then, the cultivation of a mindset of peace based on justice, on respect for the rights and duties of all, and on commitment to cooperation for the common good. And also perseverance, perseverance in good and in the rejection of evil. Here in Bethlehem, a special perseverance is asked of Christ's disciples: perseverance in faithful witness to God's glory revealed here, in the birth of his Son, to the good news of his peace that came down from heaven to dwell upon the earth.

"Do not be afraid!" This is the message that the Successor

of Saint Peter wishes to leave with you today, echoing the message of the angels and the charge that our beloved Pope John Paul II left with you in the year of the Great Jubilee of Christ's birth. Count on the prayers and solidarity of your brothers and sisters in the universal Church, and work, with concrete initiatives, to consolidate your presence and to offer new possibilities to those tempted to leave. Be a bridge of dialogue and constructive cooperation in the building of a culture of peace to replace the present stalemate of fear, aggression, and frustration. Build up your local Churches, making them workshops of dialogue, tolerance, and hope, as well as solidarity and practical charity.

Above all, be witnesses to the power of life, the new life brought by the Risen Christ, the life that can illumine and transform even the darkest and most hopeless of human situations. Your homeland needs not only new economic and community structures, but most importantly, we might say, a new "spiritual" infrastructure, capable of galvanizing the energies of all men and women of goodwill in the service of education, development, and the promotion of the common good. You have the human resources to build the culture of peace and the mutual respect that will guarantee a better future for your children. This noble enterprise awaits you. Do not be afraid!

The ancient Basilica of the Nativity, buffeted by the winds of history and the burden of the ages, stands before us as a witness to the faith that endures and triumphs over the world (cf. 1 John 5:4). No visitor to Bethlehem can fail to notice that in the course of the centuries the great door leading into the house of God has become progressively smaller. Today let us pray that, by God's grace and our commitment, the door leading into the mystery of God's dwelling among men, the temple of our communion in his love, and the foretaste of a world of eternal peace and joy, will open ever more-fully to welcome, renew, and transform every human heart. In this way, Bethlehem will continue to echo the message entrusted to the shepherds, to us, and to all mankind: "Glory to God in the highest, and on earth, peace to those whom he loves!" Amen.

24

VISIT TO THE CARITAS BABY HOSPITAL, BETHLEHEM

Dear Friends,

I affectionately greet you in the name of our Lord Jesus Christ, "who died, was raised from the dead, and now sits at the right hand of God to intercede for us" (cf. Rom 8:34). May your faith in his resurrection and his promise of new life through baptism fill your hearts with joy in this Easter season!

I am grateful for the warm welcome extended to me on your behalf by Father Michael Schweiger, president of the Kinderhilfe Association, Mr. Ernesto Langensand, who is completing his term as chief administrator of the Caritas Baby Hospital, and Mother Erika Nobs, superior of this local community of the Elizabettine Franciscan Sisters of Padua. I also cordially greet Archbishop Robert Zollitsch and Bishop Kurt Koch, representing respectively the German and Swiss Episcopal Conferences, which have advanced the mission of Caritas Baby Hospital by their generous financial assistance.

God has blessed me with this opportunity to express my appreciation to the administrators, physicians, nurses, and staff of Caritas Baby Hospital for the invaluable service they have offered—and continue to offer—to children in the Bethlehem region and throughout Palestine for over fifty years. Father Ernst Schnydrig founded this facility upon the conviction that innocent children deserve a safe haven from all that can harm them in times and places of conflict. Thanks to the dedication of Children's Relief Bethlehem, this institution has remained a quiet oasis for the most vulnerable and has shone as a beacon of hope that love can prevail over hatred and peace over violence.

To the young patients and the members of their families who benefit from your care, I wish simply to say: "The Pope is with you!" Today he is with you in person, but he spiritually accompanies you each and every day in his thoughts and prayers, asking the Almighty to watch over you with his tender care.

Father Schnydrig described this place as "one of the smaller bridges built for peace." Now, having grown from fourteen cots to eighty beds, and caring for the needs of thousands of children each year, this bridge is no longer small! It brings together people of different origins, languages, and religions, in the name of the Reign of God, the Kingdom of Peace (cf. Rom 14:17). I heartily encourage you to persevere in your mission of showing charity to all the sick, the poor, and the weak.

On this Feast of Our Lady of Fatima, I would like to conclude by invoking Mary's intercession as I impart my apostolic blessing to the children and all of you. Let us pray:

Mary, Health of the Sick, Refuge of Sinners, Mother of the Redeemer:
 We join the many generations who have called you "Blessed." Listen to your children as we call upon your name.

You promised the three children of Fatima that "in the end, my Immaculate Heart will triumph." May it be so!

May love triumph over hatred, solidarity over division, and peace over every form of violence! May the love you bore your Son teach us to love God with all our heart, strength, and soul. May the Almighty show us his mercy, strengthen us with his power, and fill us with every good thing (cf. Luke 1:46–56).

We ask your Son Jesus to bless these children and all children who suffer throughout the world. May they receive health of body, strength of mind, and peace of soul. But most of all, may they know that they are loved with a love which knows no bounds or limits: the love of Christ which surpasses all understanding (cf. Eph 3:19).

Amen.

25

VISIT TO THE AIDA REFUGEE CAMP, BETHLEHEM

Mr. President,
Dear Friends,

My visit to the Aida Refugee Camp this afternoon gives me a welcome opportunity to express my solidarity with all the homeless Palestinians who long to be able to return to their birthplace, or to live permanently in a homeland of their own. Thank you, Mr. President, for your kind greeting. And thank you also, Mrs. Abu Zayd, and our other speakers. To all the officials of the United Nations Relief and Works Agency who care for the refugees, I express the appreciation felt by countless men and women all over the world for the work that is done here and in other camps throughout the region.

I extend a particular greeting to the pupils and teachers in the school. By your commitment to education you are expressing hope in the future. To all the young people here, I say: renew your efforts to prepare for the time when you will be responsible for the affairs of the Palestinian people in years to come. Parents have a most important role here, and to all the families present in this camp I say: be sure to support your children in their studies and to nurture their gifts, so that there will be no shortage of well-qualified personnel to occupy leadership positions in the Palestinian community in the future. I know that many of your families are divided—through imprisonment of family members, or restrictions on freedom of movement—and many of you have experienced bereavement in the course of the hostilities. My heart goes out to all who suffer in this way. Please be assured that all Palestinian refugees across the world, especially those who lost homes and loved ones during the recent conflict in Gaza, are constantly remembered in my prayers.

I wish to acknowledge the good work carried out by many Church agencies in caring for refugees here and in other parts of the Palestinian Territories. The Pontifical Mission for Palestine, founded some sixty years ago to coordinate Catholic humanitarian assistance for refugees, continues its much-needed work alongside other such organizations. In this camp, the presence of Franciscan Missionary Sisters of the Immaculate Heart of Mary calls to mind the charismatic figure of Saint Francis, that great apostle of peace and reconciliation. Indeed, I want to express my particular appreciation for the enormous contribution made by different members of the Franciscan family in caring for the people of these lands, making themselves "instruments of peace," in the time-honored phrase attributed to the Saint of Assisi.

Instruments of peace. How much the people of this camp, these Territories, and this entire region long for peace! In these days, that longing takes on a particular poignancy as you recall the events of May 1948 and the years of conflict, as yet unresolved, that followed from those events. You are now living in precarious and difficult conditions, with limited opportunities for employment. It is understandable that you often feel frustrated. Your legitimate aspirations for permanent homes, for an independent Palestinian State, remain unfulfilled. Instead, you find yourselves trapped, as so many in this region and throughout the world are trapped, in a spiral of violence, attack and counterattack, retaliation, and continual destruction. The whole world is longing for this spiral to be broken, for peace to put an end to the constant fighting.

Towering over us, as we gather here this afternoon, is a stark reminder of the stalemate that relations between Israelis and Palestinians seem to have reached—the wall. In a world where more and more borders are being opened up—to trade, to travel, to movement of peoples, to cultural exchanges—it is tragic to see walls still being erected. How we long to see the fruits of the much more difficult task of building peace! How earnestly we pray for an end to the hostilities that have caused this wall to be built!

On both sides of the wall, great courage is needed if fear and mistrust is to be overcome, if the urge to retaliate for loss or injury is to be resisted. It takes magnanimity to seek reconciliation after years of fighting. Yet history has shown that peace can only come when the parties to a conflict are willing to move beyond their grievances and work together toward common goals, each taking seriously the concerns and fears of the other, striving to build an atmosphere of trust. There has to be a willingness to take bold and imaginative initiatives toward reconciliation: if each insists on prior concessions from the other, the result can only be stalemate.

Humanitarian aid, of the kind provided in this camp, has an essential role to play, but the long-term solution to a conflict such as this can only be political. No one expects the Palestinian and Israeli peoples to arrive at it on their own. The support of the international community is vital, and hence I make a renewed appeal to all concerned to bring their influence to bear in favor of a just and lasting solution, respecting the legitimate demands of all parties and recognizing their right to live in peace and dignity, in accordance with international law. Yet at the same time, diplomatic efforts can only succeed if Palestinians and Israelis themselves are willing to break free from the cycle of aggression. I am reminded of those other beautiful words attributed to Saint Francis: "Where there is hatred, let me sow love; where there is injury, pardon;...where there is darkness, light; where there is sadness, joy."

To all of you I renew my plea for a profound commitment to cultivate peace and nonviolence, following the example of Saint Francis and other great peacemakers. Peace has to begin in the home, in the family, in the heart. I continue to pray that all parties to the conflict in these lands will have the courage and imagination to pursue the challenging but indispensable path of reconciliation. May peace flourish once more in these lands! May God bless his people with peace!

26

FAREWELL CEREMONY IN THE COURTYARD OF THE PRESIDENTIAL PALACE, BETHLEHEM

Mr. President,
Dear Friends,

I thank you for the great kindness you have shown me throughout this day that I have spent in your company, here in the Palestinian Territories. I am grateful to the president, Mr. Mahmoud Abbas, for his hospitality and his gracious words. It was deeply moving for me to listen also to the testimonies of the residents who have spoken to us about the conditions of life here on the West Bank and in Gaza. I assure all of you that I hold you in my heart and I long to see peace and reconciliation throughout these tormented lands.

It has truly been a most memorable day. Since arriving in Bethlehem this morning, I have had the joy of celebrating Mass together with a great multitude of the faithful in the place where Jesus Christ, light of the nations and hope of the world, was born. I have seen the care taken of today's infants in the Caritas Baby Hospital. With anguish, I have witnessed the situation of refugees who, like the Holy Family, have had to flee their homes. And I have seen, adjoining the camp and overshadowing much of Bethlehem, the wall that intrudes into your territories, separating neighbors and dividing families.

Although walls can easily be built, we all know that they do not last forever. They can be taken down. First,

Day Six: May 13, 2009

though, it is necessary to remove the walls that we build around our hearts, the barriers that we set up against our neighbors. That is why, in my parting words, I want to make a renewed plea for openness and generosity of spirit, for an end to intolerance and exclusion. No matter how intractable and deeply entrenched a conflict may appear to be, there are always grounds to hope that it can be resolved, that the patient and persevering efforts of those who work for peace and reconciliation will bear fruit in the end. My earnest wish for you, the people of Palestine, is that this will happen soon, and that you will at last be able to enjoy the peace, freedom, and stability that have eluded you for so long.

Be assured that I will continue to take every opportunity to urge those involved in peace negotiations to work toward a just solution that respects the legitimate aspirations of Israelis and Palestinians alike. As an important step in this direction, the Holy See looks forward to establishing shortly, in conjunction with the Palestinian Authority, the Bilateral Permanent Working Commission that was envisioned in the Basic Agreement, signed in the Vatican on 15 February 2000 (cf. Basic Agreement between the Holy See and the Palestine Liberation Organization, art. 9).

Mr. President, dear friends, I thank you once again and I commend all of you to the protection of the Almighty. May God look down in love upon each one of you, upon your families and all who are dear to you. And may he bless the Palestinian people with peace.

107

Day Seven

May 14, 2009

27

HOMILY AT MASS CELEBRATED AT THE MOUNT OF PRECIPICE, NAZARETH

Dear Brothers and Sisters,

"May the peace of the Risen Christ reign in your hearts, for as members of the one body you have been called to that peace!" (Col 3:15). With these words of the Apostle Paul, I greet all of you with affection in the Lord. I rejoice to have come to Nazareth, the place blessed by the mystery of the annunciation, the place which witnessed the hidden years of Christ's growth in wisdom, age, and grace (cf. Luke 2:52). I thank Archbishop Elias Chacour for his kind words of welcome, and I embrace with the sign of peace my brother bishops, the priests and religious, and all the faithful of Galilee, who, in the diversity of their rites and traditions, give expression to the universality of Christ's Church. In a special way, I wish to thank all those who have helped to make this celebration possible, particularly those involved in the planning and construction of this new theater with its splendid panorama of the city.

Here in the hometown of Jesus, Mary, and Joseph, we have gathered to mark the conclusion of the Year of the Family celebrated by the Church in the Holy Land. As a sign of hope for the future, I will bless the first stone of an International Center for the Family to be built in Nazareth.

Let us pray that the Center will promote strong family life in this region, offer support and assistance to families everywhere, and encourage them in their irreplaceable mission to society.

This stage of my pilgrimage, I am confident, will draw the whole Church's attention to this town of Nazareth. All of us need, as Pope Paul VI said here, to return to Nazareth, to contemplate ever anew the silence and love of the Holy Family, the model of all Christian family life. Here, in the example of Mary, Joseph, and Jesus, we come to appreciate even more fully the sacredness of the family, which in God's plan is based on the lifelong fidelity of a man and a woman consecrated by the marriage covenant and accepting of God's gift of new life. How much the men and women of our time need to reappropriate this fundamental truth, which stands at the foundation of society! And how important is the witness of married couples for the formation of sound consciences and the building of a civilization of love!

In today's first reading, drawn from the book of Sirach 3:3–7, 14–17, the word of God presents the family as the first school of wisdom, a school which trains its members in the practice of those virtues which make for authentic happiness and lasting fulfillment. In God's plan for the family, the love of husband and wife bears fruit in new life and finds daily expression in the loving efforts of parents to ensure an integral human and spiritual formation for their children. In the family each person, whether the smallest child or the oldest relative, is valued for himself or herself, and not seen simply as a means to some other end. Here we begin to glimpse something of the essential role of the family as the first building block of a well-ordered and welcoming society. We also come to appreciate, within the wider community, the duty of the State to support families in their mission of education, to protect the institution of the family and its inherent rights, and to ensure that all families can live and flourish in conditions of dignity.

The Apostle Paul, writing to the Colossians, speaks instinctively of the family when he wishes to illustrate the virtues that build up the "one body," which is the Church. As "God's chosen ones, holy and beloved," we are called to live in harmony and peace with one another, showing above all forbearance and forgiveness, with love as the highest bond of perfection (cf. Col 3:12–14). Just as in the marriage covenant, the love of man and woman is raised by grace to become a sharing in, and an expression of, the love of Christ and the Church (cf. Eph 5:32), so too the family, grounded in that love, is called to be a "domestic church," a place of faith, of prayer, and of loving concern for the true and enduring good of each of its members.

As we reflect on these realities here, in the town of the annunciation, our thoughts naturally turn to Mary, "full of grace," the mother of the Holy Family and our Mother. Nazareth reminds us of our need to acknowledge and respect the God-given dignity and proper role of women, as well as their particular charisms and talents. Whether as mothers in families, as a vital presence in the work force and the institutions of society, or in the particular vocation of following our Lord by the evangelical counsels of chastity, poverty, and obedience, women have an indispensable role in creating that "human ecology" (cf. *Centesimus Annus*, 39) which our world, and this land, so urgently needs: a milieu in which children learn to love and to cherish others, to be honest and respectful to all, to practice the virtues of mercy and forgiveness.

Here, too, we think of Saint Joseph, the just man whom God wished to place over his household. From Joseph's strong and fatherly example, Jesus learned the virtues of a manly piety, fidelity to one's word, integrity, and hard work. In the carpenter of Nazareth, he saw how authority placed at the service of love is infinitely more fruitful than the power which seeks to dominate. How much our world needs the example, guidance, and quiet strength of men like Joseph!

Finally, in contemplating the Holy Family of Nazareth, we turn to the child Jesus, who in the home of Mary and Joseph grew in wisdom and understanding, until the day he began his public ministry. Here I would simply like to leave a particular thought with the young people. The Second Vatican Council teaches that children have a special role to play in the growth of their parents in holiness (cf. *Gaudium et Spes*, 48). I urge you to reflect on this, and to let the example of Jesus guide you, not only in showing respect for your parents, but also helping them to discover more fully the love that gives our lives their deepest meaning. In the Holy Family of Nazareth, it was Jesus who taught Mary and Joseph something of the greatness of the love of God his heavenly Father, the ultimate source of all love, the Father from whom every family in heaven and on earth takes its name (cf. Eph 3:14–15).

Dear friends, in the Opening Prayer of today's Mass we asked the Father to "help us to live as the Holy Family, united in respect and love." Let us reaffirm here our commitment to be a leaven of respect and love in the world around us. This Mount of the Precipice reminds us, as it has generations of pilgrims, that our Lord's message was at times a source of contradiction and conflict with his hearers. Sadly, as the world knows, Nazareth has experienced tensions in recent years that have harmed relations between its Christian and Muslim communities. I urge people of goodwill in both communities to repair the damage that has been done and, in fidelity to our common belief in one God, the Father of the human family, to work to build bridges and find the way to a peaceful coexistence. Let everyone reject the destructive power of hatred and prejudice, which kills men's souls before it kills their bodies!

Allow me to conclude with a word of gratitude and praise for all those who strive to bring God's love to the children of this town, and to educate new generations in the ways of peace. I think in a special way of the local Churches, particularly in their schools and charitable institutions, to break down walls and to be a seedbed of encounter, dialogue, reconciliation, and solidarity. I encourage the dedicated priests, religious, catechists, and teachers, together with parents and all concerned for the good of our children, to persevere in bearing witness to the Gospel, to be confident in the triumph of goodness and truth, and to trust that God will give growth to every initiative that aims at the extension of his Kingdom of holiness, solidarity, justice, and peace. At the same time I acknowledge with gratitude the solidarity that so many of our brothers and sisters throughout the world show toward the faithful of the Holy Land by supporting the praiseworthy programs and activities of the Catholic Near East Welfare Association.

"Let it be done to me according to your word" (Luke 1:38). May our Lady of the Annunciation, who courageously opened her heart to God's mysterious plan and became the Mother of all believers, guide and sustain us by her prayers. May she obtain for us and our families the grace to open our ears to that word of the Lord which has the power to build us up (cf. Acts 20:32), to inspire courageous decisions, and to guide our feet into the path of peace!

Pope Benedict XVI meets Israel's Prime Minister Benjamin Netanyahu in the northern city of Nazareth, May 14, 2009.

28

GREETINGS TO RELIGIOUS LEADERS OF GALILEE IN THE AUDITORIUM OF THE SHRINE OF THE ANNUNCIATION, NAZARETH

Dear Friends,

Grateful for the words of welcome offered by Bishop Giacinto-Boulos Marcuzzo and for your warm reception, I cordially greet the leaders of different communities present, including Christians, Muslims, Jews, Druze, and other religious peoples.

I feel particularly blessed to visit this city revered by Christians as the place where the angel announced to the

Virgin Mary that she would conceive by the power of the Holy Spirit. Here too Joseph, her betrothed, saw the angel in a dream and was directed to name the child "Jesus." After the marvelous events surrounding his birth, the child was brought to this city by Joseph and Mary where he "grew and became strong, filled with wisdom; and the favor of God was upon him" (Luke 2:40).

The conviction that the world is a gift of God, and that God has entered the twists and turns of human history, is the perspective from which Christians view creation as having a reason and a purpose. Far from being the result of blind fate, the world has been willed by God and bespeaks his glorious splendor.

At the heart of all religious traditions is the conviction that peace itself is a gift from God, yet it cannot be achieved without human endeavor. Lasting peace flows from the recognition that the world is ultimately not our own, but rather the horizon within which we are invited to participate in God's love and cooperate in guiding the world and history under his inspiration. We cannot do whatever we please with the world; rather, we are called to conform our choices to the subtle yet nonetheless perceptible laws inscribed by the Creator upon the universe and pattern our actions after the divine goodness that pervades the created realm.

Galilee, a land known for its religious and ethnic diversity, is home to a people who know well the efforts required to live in harmonious coexistence. Our different religious traditions have a powerful potential to promote a culture of peace—especially through teaching and preaching the deeper spiritual values of our common humanity. By molding the hearts of the young, we mold the future of humanity itself. Christians readily join Jews, Muslims, Druze, and people of other religions in wishing to safeguard children from fanaticism and violence while preparing them to be builders of a better world.

My dear friends, I know that you accept cheerfully and with a greeting of peace the many pilgrims who flock to Galilee. I encourage you to continue exercising mutual respect as you work to ease tensions concerning places of worship, thus assuring a serene environment for prayer and reflection here and throughout Galilee. Representing different religious traditions, you share a desire to contribute to the betterment of society and thus testify to the religious and spiritual values that help sustain public life. I assure you that the Catholic Church is committed to join in this noble undertaking. In cooperation with men and women of goodwill, she will seek to ensure that the light of truth, peace, and goodness continues to shine forth from Galilee and lead people across the globe to seek all that fosters the unity of the human family. God bless you all.

29

CELEBRATION OF VESPERS WITH BISHOPS, PRIESTS, MEN AND WOMEN RELIGIOUS, AND ECCLESIAL AND PASTORAL MOVEMENTS OF GALILEE, IN THE UPPER BASILICA OF THE ANNUNCIATION, NAZARETH

Brother Bishops,
Father Custos,
Dear Brothers and Sisters in Christ,

It is profoundly moving for me to be present with you today in the very place where the Word of God was made flesh and came to dwell among us. How fitting that we should gather here to sing the Evening Prayer of the Church, giving praise and thanks to God for the marvels he has done for us! I thank Archbishop Sayah for his words of welcome and through him I greet all the members of the Maronite community here in the Holy Land. I greet the priests, religious, members of ecclesial movements, and pastoral workers from all over Galilee. Once again I pay tribute to the care shown by the Friars of the Custody, over many centuries, in maintaining holy places such as this. I greet the Latin Patriarch Emeritus, His Beatitude Michel Sabbah, who for more than twenty years presided over his flock in these lands. I greet the faithful of the Latin Patriarchate and their current Patriarch, His Beatitude Fouad Twal, as well as the members of the Greek-Melkite community, represented here by Archbishop Elias Chacour. And in this place where Jesus himself grew to maturity and learned the Hebrew tongue, I greet the Hebrew-speaking Christians, a reminder to us of the Jewish roots of our faith.

What happened here in Nazareth, far from the gaze of the world, was a singular act of God, a powerful intervention in history, through which a child was conceived who was to bring salvation to the whole world. The wonder of the Incarnation continues to challenge us to open up our understanding to the limitless possibilities of God's transforming power, of his love for us, of his desire to be united with us. Here the eternally begotten Son of God became man, and so made it possible for us, his brothers and sisters, to share in his divine sonship. That downward movement of self-emptying love made possible the upward movement of exaltation in which we too are raised to share in the life of God himself (cf. Phil 2:6–11).

The Spirit who "came upon Mary" (cf. Luke 1:35) is the same Spirit who hovered over the waters at the dawn of Creation (cf. Gen 1:2). We are reminded that the Incarnation was a new creative act. When our Lord Jesus Christ was conceived in Mary's virginal womb through the power of the Holy Spirit, God united himself with our created humanity, entering into a permanent new relationship with us and ushering in a new Creation. The narrative of the annunciation illustrates God's extraordinary courtesy (cf. Mother Julian of Norwich, *Revelations*, 77–79). He does not impose himself, he does not simply predetermine the part that Mary will play in his plan for our salvation: he first seeks her consent. In the original Creation, there was clearly no question of God seeking the consent of his creatures, but in this new Creation he does so. Mary stands in the place of all humanity. She speaks for us all when she responds to the angel's invitation. Saint Bernard describes how the whole court of heaven was waiting with eager anticipation for her word of consent that consummated the nuptial union between God and humanity. The attention of all the choirs of angels was riveted on this spot, where a dialogue took place that would launch a new and definitive chapter in world history. Mary said, "Let it be done to me according to your word." And the Word of God became flesh.

When we reflect on this joyful mystery, it gives us hope, the sure hope that God will continue to reach into our history, to act with creative power so as to achieve goals which, by human reckoning, seem impossible. It challenges us to open ourselves to the transforming action of the Creator Spirit who makes us new, makes us one with him, and fills us with his life. It invites us, with exquisite courtesy, to consent to his dwelling within us, to welcome the Word of God into our hearts, enabling us to respond to him in love and to reach out in love toward one another.

In the State of Israel and the Palestinian Territories, Christians form a minority of the population. Perhaps at times you feel that your voice counts for little. Many of your fellow Christians have emigrated, in the hope of finding greater security and better prospects elsewhere. Your situation calls to mind that of the young virgin Mary, who led a hidden life in Nazareth, with little by way of worldly wealth or influence. Yet to quote Mary's words in her great hymn of praise, the *Magnificat*, God has looked upon his servant in her lowliness; he has filled the hungry with good things.

Draw strength from Mary's canticle, which very soon we will be singing in union with the whole Church throughout the world! Have the confidence to be faithful to Christ and to remain here in the land that he sanctified with his own presence! Like Mary, you have a part to play in God's plan for salvation: by bringing Christ forth into the world, by bearing witness to him, and by spreading his message of peace and unity. For this, it is essential that you should be united among yourselves, so that the Church in the Holy Land can be clearly recognized as "a sign and instrument of communion with God and of the unity of the entire human race" (*Lumen Gentium*, 1). Your unity in faith, hope, and love is a fruit of the Holy Spirit dwelling within you, enabling you to be effective instruments of God's peace, helping to build genuine reconciliation between the different peoples who recognize Abraham as their father in faith. For, as Mary joyfully proclaimed in her *Magnificat*, God is ever "mindful of his mercy, the mercy promised to our forefathers, to Abraham and his children forever" (Luke 1:54–55).

Dear friends in Christ, be assured that I constantly remember you in my prayer, and I ask you to do the same for me. Let us turn now toward our heavenly Father, who in this place looked upon his servant in her lowliness, and let us sing his praises in union with the Blessed Virgin Mary, with all the choirs of angels and saints, and with the whole Church in every part of the world.

Day Eight

May 15, 2009

30

ADDRESS GIVEN AT AN ECUMENICAL MEETING IN THE THRONE HALL OF THE GREEK ORTHODOX PATRIARCHATE, JERUSALEM

Dear Brothers and Sisters in Christ,

It is with profound gratitude and joy that I make this visit to the Greek Orthodox Patriarchate of Jerusalem, a moment I have much anticipated. I thank His Beatitude Patriarch Theophilus III for his kind words of fraternal greeting, which I warmly reciprocate. I also express to all of you my heartfelt gratitude for providing me with this opportunity to meet once again the many leaders of Churches and ecclesial communities present.

This morning I am mindful of the historic meetings that have taken place here in Jerusalem between my predecessor Pope Paul VI and the Ecumenical Patriarch Athenagoras I, and also between Pope John Paul II and His Beatitude Patriarch Diodoros. These encounters, including my visit today, are of great symbolic significance. They recall that the light of the East (cf. Isa 60:1; Rev 21:10) has illumined the entire world from the very moment when a "rising sun" came to visit us (Luke 1:78), and they remind us too that from here the Gospel was preached to all nations.

Standing in this hallowed place, alongside the Church of the Holy Sepulcher, which marks the site where our crucified Lord rose from the dead for all humanity, and near the Cenacle, where on the day of Pentecost "they were all together in one place" (Acts 2:1), who could not feel impelled to bring the fullness of goodwill, sound scholarship, and spiritual desire to our ecumenical endeavors? I pray that our gathering today will give new impetus to the work of theological dialogue between the Catholic Church and the Orthodox Churches, adding to the recent fruits of study documents and other joint initiatives.

Of particular joy for our Churches has been the participation of the Ecumenical Patriarch of Constantinople, His Holiness Bartholomew I, at the recent Synod of Bishops in Rome dedicated to the theme: *The Word of God in the Life and Mission of the Church*. The warm welcome he received and his moving intervention were sincere expressions of the deep spiritual joy that arises from the extent to which communion is already present between our Churches. Such ecumenical experience bears clear witness to the link between the unity of the Church and her mission. Extending his arms on the Cross, Jesus revealed the fullness of his desire to draw all people to himself, uniting them together as one (cf. John 12:32). Breathing his Spirit upon us he revealed his power to enable us to participate in his mission of reconciliation (cf. John 19:30; 20:22–23). In that breath, through the redemption that unites, stands our mission! Little wonder, then, that it is precisely in our burning desire to bring Christ to others, to make known his message of reconciliation (cf. 2 Cor 5:19), that we experience the shame of our division. Yet, sent out into the world (cf. John 20:21), empowered by the unifying force of the Holy Spirit (John 20:22), proclaiming the reconciliation that draws all to believe that Jesus is the Son of God

(John 20:31), we shall find the strength to redouble our efforts to perfect our communion, to make it complete, to bear united witness to the love of the Father who sends the Son so that the world may know his love for us (cf. John 17:23).

Some two thousand years ago, along these same streets, a group of Greeks put this request to Philip: "Sir, we should like to see Jesus" (John 12:21). It is a request made again of us today, here in Jerusalem, in the Holy Land, in the region and throughout the world. How do we respond? Is our response heard? Saint Paul alerts us to the gravity of our response: our mission to teach and preach. He says: "Faith comes from hearing, and what is heard comes through the word of Christ" (Rom 10:17). It is imperative therefore that Christian leaders and their communities bear vibrant testimony to what our faith proclaims: the eternal Word, who entered space and time in this land, Jesus of Nazareth, who walked these streets, through his words and actions calls people of every age to his life of truth and love.

Dear friends, while encouraging you to proclaim joyfully the Risen Lord, I wish also to recognize the work to this end of the heads of Christian communities, who meet together regularly in this city. It seems to me that the greatest service the Christians of Jerusalem can offer their fellow citizens is the upbringing and education of a further generation of well-formed and committed Christians, earnest in their desire to contribute generously to the religious and civic life of this unique and holy city. The fundamental priority of every Christian leader is the nurturing of the faith of the individuals and families entrusted to his pastoral care. This common pastoral concern will ensure that your regular meetings are marked by the wisdom and fraternal charity necessary to support one another and to engage with both the joys and the particular difficulties that mark the lives of your people. I pray that the aspirations of the Christians of Jerusalem will be understood as being concordant with the aspirations of all its inhabitants, whatever their religion: a life of religious freedom and peaceful coexistence and—for young people in particular—unimpeded access to education and employment, the prospect of suitable housing and family residency, and the chance to benefit from and contribute to economic stability.

Your Beatitude, I thank you again for your kindness in inviting me here, together with the other guests. Upon each of you and the communities you represent, I invoke an abundance of God's blessings of fortitude and wisdom! May you all be strengthened by the hope of Christ, which does not disappoint!

3 1

VISIT TO THE HOLY SEPULCHER

Dear Friends in Christ,

The hymn of praise which we have just sung unites us with the angelic hosts and the Church of every time and place—"the glorious company of the apostles, the noble fellowship of the prophets, and the white-robed army of martyrs"—as we give glory to God for the work of our redemption, accomplished in the passion, death, and resurrection of Jesus Christ. Before this Holy Sepulcher, where the Lord "overcame the sting of death and opened the kingdom of heaven to all believers," I greet all of you in the joy of the Easter season. I thank Patriarch Fouad Twal and the Custos, Father Pierbattista Pizzaballa, for their kind greeting. I likewise express my appreciation for the reception accorded me by the Hierarchs of the Greek Orthodox Church and the Armenian Apostolic Church. I gratefully acknowledge the presence of representatives of the other Christian communities in the Holy Land. I greet Cardinal John Foley, Grand Master of the Equestrian Order of the Holy Sepulcher, and also the Knights and Ladies of the Order here present, with gratitude for their unfailing commitment to the support of the Church's mission in these lands made holy by the Lord's earthly presence.

Saint John's Gospel has left us an evocative account of the visit of Peter and the Beloved Disciple to the empty tomb on Easter morning. Today, at a distance of some twenty centuries, Peter's Successor, the Bishop of Rome, stands before that same empty tomb and contemplates the mystery of the resurrection. Following in the footsteps of the Apostle, I wish to proclaim anew, to the men and women of our time, the Church's firm faith that Jesus Christ "was crucified, died, and was buried," and that "on the third day he rose from the dead." Exalted at the right hand of the Father, he has sent us his Spirit for the forgiveness of sins. Apart from him, whom God has made Lord and Christ, "there is no other name under heaven given to men by which we are to be saved" (Acts 4:12).

Standing in this holy place, and pondering that wondrous event, how can we not be "cut to the heart" (Acts 2:37), like those who first heard Peter's preaching on the day of Pentecost? Here Christ died and rose, never to die again. Here the history of humanity was decisively changed. The long reign of sin and death was shattered by the triumph of obedience and life; the wood of the Cross lay bare the truth about good and evil; God's judgment was passed on this world and the grace of the Holy Spirit was poured out upon humanity. Here Christ, the new Adam, taught us that evil never has the last word, that love is stronger than death, that our future, and the future of all humanity, lies in the hands of a faithful and provident God.

The empty tomb speaks to us of hope, the hope that does not disappoint because it is the gift of the Spirit of life (cf. Rom 5:5). This is the message that I wish to leave with you today, at the conclusion of my pilgrimage to the Holy Land. May hope rise up ever anew, by God's grace, in the hearts of all the people dwelling in these lands! May it take root in your hearts, abide in your families and communities, and inspire in each of you an ever more-faithful witness to the Prince of Peace! The Church in the Holy Land, which has so often experienced the dark mystery of Golgotha, must never cease to be an intrepid herald of the luminous message of hope that this empty tomb proclaims. The Gospel reassures us that God can make all things new, that history need not be repeated, that memories can be healed, that the bitter fruits of recrimination, and hostility can be overcome, and that a future of justice, peace, prosperity, and cooperation can arise for every man and woman, for the whole human family, and in a special way for the people who dwell in this land so dear to the heart of the Savior.

This ancient Memorial of the Anástasis bears mute witness both to the burden of our past, with its failings, misunderstandings, and conflicts, and to the glorious promise that continues to radiate from Christ's empty tomb. This holy place, where God's power was revealed in weakness, and human sufferings were transfigured by divine glory, invites us to look once again with the eyes of faith upon the face of the crucified and Risen Lord. Contemplating his glorified flesh, completely transfigured by the Spirit, may we come to realize more fully that even now, through baptism, "we bear in our bodies the death of Jesus, that the life of Jesus may be manifested in our own mortal flesh" (2 Cor 4:10–11). Even now, the grace of the resurrection is at work within us! May our contemplation of this mystery spur our efforts, both as individuals and as members of the ecclesial community, to grow in the life of the Spirit through conversion, penance, and prayer. May it help us to overcome, by the power of that same Spirit, every conflict and tension born of the flesh, and to remove every obstacle, both within and without, standing in the way of our common witness to Christ and the reconciling power of his love.

With these words of encouragement, dear friends, I conclude my pilgrimage to the holy places of our redemption and rebirth in Christ. I pray that the Church in the Holy Land will always draw new strength from its contemplation of the empty tomb of the Savior. In that tomb it is called to bury all its anxieties and fears, in order to rise again each day and continue its journey through the streets of Jerusalem, Galilee, and beyond, proclaiming the triumph of Christ's forgiveness and the promise of new life. As Christians, we know that the peace for which this strife-torn land yearns has a name: Jesus Christ. "He is our peace," who reconciled us to God in one body through the Cross, bringing an end to hostility (cf. Eph 2:14). Into his hands, then, let us entrust all our hope for the future, just as in the hour of darkness he entrusted his spirit into the Father's hands.

Allow me to conclude with a special word of fraternal encouragement to my brother bishops and priests, and to the men and women religious who serve the beloved Church in the Holy Land. Here, before the empty tomb, at the very heart of the Church, I invite you to rekindle the enthusiasm of your consecration to Christ and your commitment to loving service of his mystical Body. Yours is the immense privilege of bearing witness to Christ in this, the land which he sanctified by his earthly presence and ministry. In pastoral charity, enable your brothers and sisters, and all the inhabitants of this land, to feel the healing presence and the reconciling love of the

Risen One. Jesus asks each of us to be a witness of unity and peace to all those who live in this City of Peace.

As the new Adam, Christ is the source of the unity to which the whole human family is called, that unity of which the Church is the sign and sacrament.

As the Lamb of God, he is the source of that reconciliation which is both God's gift and a sacred task enjoined upon us.

As the Prince of Peace, he is the source of that peace which transcends all understanding, the peace of the new Jerusalem.

May he sustain you in your trials, comfort you in your afflictions, and confirm you in your efforts to proclaim and extend his Kingdom. To all of you, and to those whom you serve, I cordially impart my apostolic blessing as a pledge of Easter joy and peace.

32

VISIT TO THE ARMENIAN PATRIARCHAL CHURCH OF ST. JAMES, JERUSALEM

Your Beatitude,

I greet you with fraternal affection in the Lord, and I offer prayerful good wishes for your health and your ministry. I am grateful for the opportunity to visit this Cathedral Church of Saint James in the heart of the ancient Armenian quarter of Jerusalem, and to meet the distinguished clergy of the Patriarchate, together with the members of the Armenian community of the Holy City.

Our meeting today, characterized by an atmosphere of cordiality and friendship, is another step along the path toward the unity that the Lord desires for all his disciples. In recent decades we have witnessed, by God's grace, a significant growth in the relationship between the Catholic Church and the Armenian Apostolic Church. I count it a great blessing to have met in this past year with the Supreme Patriarch and Catholicos of All Armenians, Karekin II, and with the Catholicos of Cilicia, Aram I. Their visits to the Holy See, and the moments of prayer which we shared, have strengthened us in fellowship and confirmed our commitment to the sacred cause of promoting Christian unity.

In a spirit of gratitude to the Lord, I wish also to express my appreciation of the unwavering commitment of the Armenian Apostolic Church to the continuing theological dialogue between the Catholic Church and the Eastern Orthodox Churches. This dialogue, sustained by prayer, has made progress in overcoming the burden of past misunderstandings, and offers much promise for the future. A particular sign of hope is the recent document on the nature and mission of the Church produced by the Mixed Commission and presented to the Churches for study and evaluation. Together let us entrust the work of the Mixed Commission once more to the Spirit of wisdom and truth, so that it can bear abundant fruit for the growth of Christian unity, and advance the spread of the Gospel among the men and women of our time.

From the first Christian centuries, the Armenian community in Jerusalem has had an illustrious history, marked not least by an extraordinary flourishing of monastic life and culture linked to the holy places and the liturgical traditions that developed around them. This venerable Cathedral Church, together with the Patriarchate and the various educational and cultural institutions attached to it, testifies to that long and distinguished history. I pray that your community will constantly draw new life from its rich traditions and be confirmed in its witness to Jesus Christ and the power of his resurrection (cf. Phil 3:10) in this Holy City. I likewise assure the families present, and particularly the children and young people, of a special remembrance in my prayers. Dear friends, I ask you in turn to pray with me that all the Christians of the Holy Land will work together with generosity and zeal in proclaiming the Gospel of our reconciliation in Christ, and the advent of his Kingdom of holiness, justice, and peace.

Your Beatitude, I thank you once more for your gracious welcome, and I cordially invoke God's richest blessings upon you and upon all the clergy and faithful of the Armenian Apostolic Church in the Holy Land. May the joy and peace of the Risen Christ be always with you.

33

DEPARTURE CEREMONY AT BEN GURION INTERNATIONAL AIRPORT, TEL AVIV

Mr. President,
Mr. Prime Minister,
Your Excellencies,
Ladies and Gentlemen,

As I prepare to return to Rome, may I share with you some of the powerful impressions that my pilgrimage to the Holy Land has left with me. I had fruitful discussions with the civil authorities both in Israel and in the Palestinian Territories, and I witnessed the great efforts that both governments are making to secure people's well-being. I have met the leaders of the Catholic Church in the Holy Land, and I rejoice to see the way that they work together in caring for the Lord's flock. I have also had the opportunity to meet the leaders of the various Christian Churches and ecclesial communities as well as the leaders of other religions in the Holy Land. This land is indeed a fertile ground for ecumenism and interreligious dialogue, and I pray that the rich variety of religious witness in the region will bear fruit in a growing mutual understanding and respect.

Mr. President, you and I planted an olive tree at your residence on the day that I arrived in Israel. The olive tree, as you know, is an image used by Saint Paul to describe the very close relations between Christians and Jews. Paul describes in his Letter to the Romans how the Church of the Gentiles is like a wild olive shoot, grafted onto the cultivated olive tree, which is the People of the Covenant (cf. Rom 11:17–24). We are nourished from the same spiritual roots. We meet as brothers, brothers who at times in our history have had a tense relationship, but now are firmly committed to building bridges of lasting friendship.

The ceremony at the Presidential Palace was followed by one of the most solemn moments of my stay in Israel: my visit to the Holocaust Memorial at Yad Vashem, where I paid my respects to the victims of the Shoah. There also I met some of the survivors. Those deeply moving encounters brought back memories of my visit three years ago to the death camp at Auschwitz, where so many Jews— mothers, fathers, husbands, wives, sons, daughters, brothers, sisters, friends—were brutally exterminated under a godless regime that propagated an ideology of anti-Semitism and hatred.

That appalling chapter of history must never be forgotten or denied. On the contrary, those dark memories should strengthen our determination to draw closer to one another as branches of the same olive tree, nourished from the same roots and united in brotherly love.

Mr. President, I thank you for the warmth of your hospitality, which is greatly appreciated, and I wish to put on record that I came to visit this country as a friend of the Israelis, just as I am a friend of the Palestinian people. Friends enjoy spending time in one another's company, and they find it deeply distressing to see one another suffer. No friend of the Israelis and the Palestinians can fail to be saddened by the continuing tension between your two peoples. No friend can fail to weep at the suffering and loss of life that both peoples have endured over the last six decades.

Allow me to make this appeal to all the people of these lands: No more bloodshed! No more fighting! No more terrorism! No more war!

Instead, let us break the vicious circle of violence. Let there be lasting peace based on justice. Let there be genuine reconciliation and healing. Let it be universally recognized that the State of Israel has the right to exist, and to enjoy peace and security within internationally agreed borders. Let it be likewise acknowledged that the Palestinian people have a right to a sovereign independent homeland, to live with dignity and to travel freely. Let the two-state solution become a reality, not remain a dream. And let peace spread outward from these lands, let them serve as a "light to the nations" (Isa 42:6), bringing hope to the many other regions that are affected by conflict.

One of the saddest sights for me during my visit to these lands was the wall. As I passed alongside it, I prayed for a future in which the peoples of the Holy Land can live together in peace and harmony without the need for such instruments of security and separation, but rather respecting and trusting one another, and renouncing all forms of violence and aggression. Mr. President, I know how hard it will be to achieve that goal. I know how difficult is your task, and that of the Palestinian Authority. But I assure you that my prayers and the prayers of Catholics across the world are with you as you continue your efforts to build a just and lasting peace in this region.

It remains only for me to express my heartfelt thanks to all who have contributed in so many ways to my visit. To the government, the organizers, the volunteers, the media, to all who have provided hospitality to me and those accompanying me, I am deeply grateful. Please be assured that you are remembered with affection in my prayers.

To all of you, I say: thank you, and may God be with you. *Shalom!*

34

INTERVIEW OF THE HOLY FATHER DURING THE FLIGHT FROM THE HOLY LAND TO ROME

Dear Friends,

Thank you for your work. I can imagine how difficult it must have been in the midst of so many problems, multiple transfers, etc. and I want to thank you for accepting all these inconveniences in order to tell the world about this pilgrimage, thereby inviting others to go on pilgrimage to these Holy Places.

Since I already made a brief summary of my journey in my speech at the airport, I do not wish to add much. I could mention many, many more details: the moving descent to the most profound spot on earth, at the River Jordan, which for us is also a symbol of the descent of God, of the descent of Christ to the deepest points of human existence.

I could mention the Upper Room, in which the Lord gave us the Eucharist, in which Pentecost, the descent of the Holy Spirit, took place; the Holy Sepulcher too, and many other impressions, but it seems to me that this is not the moment to reflect on them.

Yet perhaps I could make a few brief comments on them. There are three fundamental impressions: the first is that I found everywhere, in every context, Muslim, Christian, and Jewish, a determined readiness for interreligious dialogue, for encounter and collaboration among the religions. And it is important that everyone see this not only as an action—let us say, inspired by political motives in the given situation—but as a fruit of the very core of faith. Because believing in one God who has created us all, the Father of us all, believing in this God who created humanity as a family, believing that God is love and wants love to be the dominant force in the world, implies this encounter, this need for an encounter, for dialogue, for collaboration as a requirement of faith itself.

The second point: I also found a very encouraging ecumenical atmosphere. We had many meetings with the Orthodox world in great cordiality; I was also able to speak to a representative of the Anglican Church and two Lutheran representatives, and it is clear that this atmosphere of the Holy Land itself also encourages ecumenism.

And the third point: there are enormous difficulties, as we know, as we have seen and heard. But I also saw that there is a deep desire for peace on the part of all. The problems are more visible and we must not conceal them: they exist and need clarification. However, the common desire for peace, for brotherhood, is not so visible and it seems to me that we should also talk about this, and encourage in everyone the desire to find solutions to these problems that are certainly far from simple.

I came as a pilgrim of peace. Pilgrimage is an essential element of many religions and also of Islam, of the Jewish religion, and of Christianity. It is also the image of our existence that is moving forward toward God and hence toward the communion of humanity.

I came as a pilgrim and I hope that many will follow in my footsteps and by so doing encourage the unity of the people of this Holy Land and in turn become their messenger of peace. Thank you!

Rina Castelnuovo/REUTERS

Pope Benedict XVI plants an olive tree with Israel's President Shimon Peres at the president's residence in Jerusalem, May 11, 2009.

*Christian and Jewish
Perspectives on the
Holy Father's Visit*

35

THE HOLY FATHER IN THE HOLY LAND

Templates, Metaphors, and Expectations

Michael B. McGarry, CSP

Israeli President Shimon Peres invited him a few times. Pope Benedict XVI resisted at first, but in the end decided that, indeed, he would accept the invitation to come to the Holy Land—including the Hashemite Kingdom of Jordan, the Palestinian Authority, and the State of Israel—as a personal pilgrim. Before his election to the papacy, Joseph Ratzinger had visited the Holy Land, both to lecture as a theologian (including, in the early 1990s, at a Tantur forum on religious leadership) and to pray in retreat among Jerusalem's holy places.

His visit to the Holy Land in 2009 would be different, to be sure. This time he was coming as the Holy Father, the pope of the Roman Catholic Church, and, in Jewish and Muslim eyes, as the head of the Christian Church. In an effort to avoid misunderstanding and to stave off purely political castings of his visit, Pope Benedict insisted that he was coming to the Holy Land simply as a pilgrim with no political agenda. His words and actions in the Holy Land remained consistent with his intentions; how they were reported, however, was out of his hands. So in a few words, I wish to reflect on the pope's May 2009 journey to the Holy Land through three categories: templates, metaphors, and expectations.

TEMPLATES

Comparisons are odious, as the saying goes. Nonetheless, in answer to the question, "How does a pope visit the Holy Land?" the answer would be, "See how John Paul II did it." Maybe not odious; still, such a comparison was as unfair as it was predictable. And it formed, for many, the template for analyzing Pope Benedict in the Holy Land.

To this day, people vividly remember Pope John Paul II's iconic moments in his 2000 pilgrimage, including that gripping moment when he, the Polish pope and himself a survivor of the Nazi onslaught, grasped the outstretched hands of fellow Poles from Wadowice at Yad Vashem, Israel's museum and memorial to the Shoah. Similarly the world has etched on its memory the picture of the elderly pope shuffling to the Western Wall to insert his prayer in the crevices of the Second Temple's retaining wall.

In 2009, some asked how Benedict might be as dramatic as John Paul II. Of course, Benedict would fall short. So some local commentators described Benedict's Yad Vashem visit as "lackluster,"[1] his words as vapid, and his presence as a missed opportunity for a forceful message.[2]

But memories are short. In 2000, I clearly remember standing among Jerusalem's press gathering. Media-informed folks in Israel were on the alert to see if at Yad Vashem Pope John Paul II would "go further" than the "apology" uttered at the previous week's "Sunday of Repentance" in Rome. One veteran of Jewish-Catholic dialogue, not to be named, cursed that John Paul II "did not go far enough." Indeed at Yad Vashem, he essentially repeated what he had said in St. Peter's Basilica the week before about the sorrow the Church felt about the Shoah. And John Paul II *never* apologized. There and in similar contexts, he "expressed regret" for the failures of some of the Church's members (never of the Church itself) for mistakes from the past. So Benedict's "lackluster" talk at Yad Vashem was compared to an incorrectly remembered John Paul II talk many years before.

One prominent English-language editorial in Israel then compared Benedict's prayer inserted in the Western Wall with John Paul II's. Again, Pope Benedict's message did not pass muster.[3] Typical was Shoah historian Yehuda Bauer's observation: "The visit of John Paul II [to Israel] was an act that was hard to follow, and the present pope did his best in accordance with his personality and the tremendous pressures to which he is constantly subjected. It was not good enough....The Pope meant well, and tried to walk the tightrope....He did not quite fall off the rope, but he stumbled."[4]

While not everything that Benedict—or anyone—says can be both insightful and moving, I was wondering, as I heard the many criticisms (and defenses) of Benedict's Yad Vashem talk, how John Paul II's talk would have been evaluated if it had come after Benedict's? Impossible to know, of course, but the template of the former actor and master-of-gesture pope could only overshadow the brilliant, but bookish professor. Sadly, the template drove the commentary and not the other way around.

METAPHORS

After analyzing events within the template of the German pope (usually reminding readers of Joseph Ratzinger's forced participation in the Nazi youth corps) as compared with the Polish pope, commentators entangled themselves with two well-worn metaphors: tightrope and minefield. Both these metaphors involve missteps and stumbles. A successful visit to the Holy Land, they opined, would require that the pope not fall off during the high-wire act of speaking equally and even-handedly to and for the Palestinians and the Israelis, and the Jews, the Muslims, and the Christians. Typical of such evaluations was the National Council of Young Israel's claim that Pope Benedict "repeatedly noted his sympathy for the Palestinians with virtually no mention of the ongoing Palestinian terrorist attacks against Israeli civilians."[5]

And then there were the landmines. Jewish concerns were at least twofold: first was the Vatican's allowing the prayer for the conversion of the Jews in its newly resuscitated Tridentine Good Friday liturgy, and second was the lifting of excommunication from the Holocaust-denying Bishop Williamson. These incidents stood out against the background of Pope Benedict's own German background, which provoked many in the Israeli—and the Christian— world to see how much he would "own up" to his and the Church's past and to see "how far" he would go.

On the Muslim side, in spring 2009, one cleric in Israel said that the pope was unwelcome in Israel until he issued a full apology for his insulting the Prophet. Indeed, many in the Muslim world were still on a slow boil about the insults to the Prophet perceived in Pope Benedict's 2006 Regensburg lecture, which at the time drew strong protests and for which many felt he had never adequately apologized.

So, far from being ready to hear Pope Benedict on his

own terms and quite cognizant of these "mines in the road," the press watched with anxious eyes every step he took, every concession he made to "the Israeli side" or to "the Palestinian side," and every political nuance of his words: *Did he say "two-state solution" or only "Palestinian home-land"? Did he use the word* terrorism *or only* violence? *Did he say that the Jews were "killed" or that they were "murdered" in the death camps?* As one English editorial noted, the "mines" that the pope would step on were as much what he did not say as what he did. But the metaphors, like the templates, drove the analysis.

EXPECTATIONS

My friend Israeli Jesuit David Neuhaus used different categories from the above to describe Pope Benedict in his historic trip to the Holy Land. They were four: pilgrim, pastor, man of dialogue, and man of peace.[6] I think that Fr. Neuhaus has presented a very important alternative prism through which Pope Benedict's visit to the Holy Land should be viewed. And I think this for two reasons: first, they are the categories the pope himself chose and, second, they were the themes that thoroughly informed all his talks and homilies.

As I have read over all the talks which Pope Benedict delivered in Jordan, Israel, and the Palestinian Territories, I am impressed by the consistent emphasis he put on how he understood his own trip—as a pilgrim, as someone who has come to pray for peace in a land torn by strife, and as a person passionately solicitous of all the people who live in this troubled land.

In his talks with Muslims (mostly in Jordan), he emphasized Christian and Muslim shared values and the common ground from which Christians and Muslims approach each other as children of the one God. In his talks with the Jewish people (obviously in Israel), he emphasized the common patrimony we share and our common destiny.

In his talks with the local Catholic Christians—in Jordan, Israel, and the Territories—he encouraged, and held up the importance of, the Christian presence in the Holy Land. God forbid, he pleaded, that the Holy Land should ever shrink into the rubble of dead stones marking the presence of a long departed faithful!

In speaking with other parts of the Christian family, Pope Benedict underscored what all Christians share and the unity all yearn for but which turns out to be so elusive. In his talks with other Christians, not surprisingly, Pope Benedict underscored the Christocentric dimension of the Christian faith—Catholic, Protestant, and Orthodox. Although not emphasized in the press, these themes of peace, unity, nonviolence, and mutual respect were fundamental to the leader of the Catholic Church as he sought both to deepen dialogical relations with Muslims and Jews and to pastor the local Church and work for Christian unity.

Finally what does "understanding a papal visit" mean? I suggest that there are at least three levels: first, there is the pope's own self-understanding; here I must emphasize that Benedict's own self description—as a pilgrim coming to pray for peace and to engage its friends on all sides—must hold pride of place. Secondly, there is the global framing of the papal journey, the "macro level." These are the analyses offered in the press, which I have—admittedly superficially—described. It is not peculiar to papal visits to the Holy Land to become trapped by templates and metaphors-of-the-moment from observers who, similarly, come from foreign soil. And thirdly, there is the local level, the perception and experience of those who live in the Holy Land.

Indeed, up to now, most of what I have written could have been discerned by anyone who follows the news by Internet and newspaper. So here I wish to reflect only on the local Christian experience—the "feel on the ground," if you will. This is always elusive, ephemeral, and influenced too much by the last person you talked to. While the first two levels are important, this third level deserves more attention that it has received.

When rumors of a papal trip to the Holy Land first surfaced, there was much talk among local Catholic Christians about the inopportuneness of the timing of the papal visit. Many local Christians are very sophisticated in their reading of the national and international press, and they feared that Pope Benedict's coming to the Holy Land would be driven and interpreted by agendas far from their daily concerns. They were aware of the recent stories about the Holocaust-denying bishop. The Shoah, for all its horror, is not part of the local indigenous Christian history. Consequently and perhaps understandably, the Western press's preoccupation with Williamson would eclipse attention to local Christian concerns. Similarly, pressures from certain Muslim forces, still smarting from the Regensburg speech, would throw a magnifying glass on all things Islamic in the papal itinerary.

Sharing her misgivings about the opportuneness of the papal visit, one local Palestinian sister offered this succinct but cryptic bit of advice: "Tell the Pope not to lose his dignity." I have thought about that advice over and over, and in its simple and multivalent dimensions, I think it reveals something quite profound. Other locals, knowing more of Israeli-Vatican diplomacy, put it more bluntly: "Tell him *not* to come until the State of Israel ceases the humiliation of not ratifying the 1993 Fundamental Accords in the Knesset."[7] The pressures that local and expatriate Christians live under are difficult, complicated, and impossible, in a short space, to describe. But local Christians, both Palestinian and internationals, feared that the potential, genuine good that can come from a papal journey would be neutralized by other agendas, namely the Western agenda of Jewish-Catholic relations and the ongoing discussion of the clash of civilizations between the West (Christianity) and Islam.

In the end, local Christians feared that their legitimate concerns would be completely eclipsed by the press's strait-jacketing its coverage to, as I have termed them, the templates and metaphors. From my perspective, the press early and easily settled into these. Fr. Neuhaus's interpreting the papal journey in a more positive light is necessary to draw attention to what the pope actually said and did. In the end, however, from my perspective, the papal speeches themselves tended toward the general and, in some cases, the platitudinous. It is difficult to remember any particular message of the pope during his weeklong pilgrimage. As one local Church leader said to me afterward, with perhaps the exception of the pope's talk at the Aida Refugee camp, any person of goodwill could agree with all the pope's speeches...which may be as it should be.

Like beauty, papal trips, then, may be in the eye of the beholder. Jesus asked of those curious about John the Baptist: "What did you go out into the wilderness to look at?" Indeed, what were *we* looking for in the Judean wilderness? Our expectations may leave us only limited possibilities for evaluating a "successful papal trip to the Holy Land." Were we Israeli Jews, waiting for an apology for the Shoah? Were we Palestinian Muslims, waiting for an apology for an insult to the Prophet? Were we Palestinian Christians, waiting for a champion for our rights and a sympathetic ear to our sufferings?

What did the pope, in his own heart, wish to accomplish? On May 15 of 2009, reflecting back on his trip to the Holy Land during his general audience in St. Peter's Square, Pope Benedict described it as:

"pilgrimage *par excellence* to the sources of the faith, and at the same time a pastoral visit to the Church that lives there…" I am happy to be able to recapitulate the entire itinerary I was able to make in the sign of Christ's resurrection. Despite the vicissitudes that over the centuries have affected the Holy Places…the Church has continued her mission, moved by the Spirit of the Risen Lord. She is on a journey to full unity, that the world may believe in the love of God and experience the joy of His peace.[8]

Michael B. McGarry, CSP, was rector of the Tantur Ecumenical Institute at the southern end of Jerusalem and the northern end of Bethlehem from September 1999 to May 2010, until he became president of the Paulist Fathers. He served the local Latin Patriarch as secretary to his commission on relations with the Jewish people. Both he and Yehezkel Landau contributed the Christian and Jewish perspectives in Pope John Paul II in the Holy Land *(Paulist Press, 2005).*

NOTES

1. See Debbie Weissman, "Lackluster Visit," *The Jerusalem Report* (June 8, 2009): 12.

2. See editorial from *Haaretz* (May 13, 2009): "His [Pope Benedict's] important statements condemning anti-Semitic and Holocaust denial lost their potency because of his lukewarm

remarks at Yad Vashem. The pope's visit shows that there is no real dialogue between Israel and the Vatican, and that it is difficult to erase centuries-old wounds."

3. For a side-by-side comparison, here is Benedict's prayer: "God of all the ages, on my visit to Jerusalem, the 'City of Peace,' spiritual home to Jews, Christians, and Muslims alike, I bring before you the joys, the hopes, and the aspirations, the trials, the suffering, and the pain, of all your people throughout the world. God of Abraham, Isaac, and Jacob, hear the cry of the afflicted, the fearful, the bereft; send your peace upon this Holy Land, upon the Middle East, upon the entire human family; stir the hearts of all who call upon your name, to walk humbly in the path of justice and compassion. 'The Lord is good to those who wait for him, to the soul that seeks him!' (Lam 3:25)."

And here is John Paul II's prayer: "God of our fathers, you chose Abraham and his descendants to bring Your name to the nations: we are deeply saddened by the behavior of those who in the course of history have caused these children of Yours to suffer and, asking Your forgiveness, we wish to commit ourselves to genuine brotherhood with the people of the Covenant. Amen."

4. Yehuda Bauer, "The Pope Meant Well," *The Jerusalem Post* (May 13, 2009).

5. See website http://www.youngisrael.org/pages/index.cfm/Young-Israel-Movement-Questions-Popes-Israel-Stance.

6. See David Neuhaus, SJ, "Benedict's visit to a land called to be holy," http://www.thinkingfaith.org/articles/20090609_1.htm.

7. See Marie-Armelle Beaulieu, "The Pope's Pilgrimage and the Agreement between the Holy See and the State of Israel," http://www.custodia.org/spip.php?article5279.

8. Vatican Information Service, May 20, 2009.

36

JEWISH PERSPECTIVES ON POPE BENEDICT XVI'S VISIT TO THE HOLY LAND

Dr. Deborah Weissman

Jewish responses to the papal visit to the Holy Land of May 2009 shed more light on Jews and Judaism than they do on the pontiff or his visit.

Jews, who were a persecuted minority in most periods and in most places, and who have sometimes been treated violently by the surrounding societies, have developed defensive, insulating postures. They often engaged in polemics with the outside world, particularly within medieval Christendom. The victimhood of Jewish history, of course, and the feeling of abject powerlessness, reached their tragic climax in the Holocaust in Europe 1933 to 1945. If many Jews today are mistrustful of the outside world, it is not without cause.

A well-known joke says, "Just because you're paranoid doesn't mean that they're not out to get you." Even paranoiacs can have real enemies. The phenomena of anti-Semitism and even neo-Nazism are still very much with us. In the Middle East, both the Israelis and the Palestinians see themselves as the victims of the conflict. They seem to be competitors in a "suffering sweepstakes." One of the problems with victimhood is that it prevents the victim from assuming responsibility for his actions, including the victimization of others. In the Israeli-Palestinian conflict, I believe that both sides are victims and both sides are victimizers.

One of the features of Jewish life that developed during the many centuries of persecution is our tendency to view all events through this rather narrow prism: "Is it good or bad for the Jews?" This tendency, coupled with a basic ignorance about Christianity on the part of many Jews, can account for several aspects of how the 2009 visit of Pope Benedict XVI to the Holy Land was experienced by Jews, and how it was compared to the 2000 visit of his predecessor, Pope John Paul II.

The difference between the two men is not only one of personal warmth and charisma. Today's pope—formerly Cardinal Joseph Ratzinger—was and remains a theology professor; his predecessor, Karol Jozef Wojtyla, had been an actor and a playwright before entering the Polish seminary, and remained the master of the symbolic gesture. However, forget that even he, in the late 1980s, was the target of much Jewish criticism for his welcome to the Vatican of former Nazi Kurt Waldheim. In retrospect, Pope John Paul II seems to have been so admired by Jews that they are unaware of the more complex and controversial aspects of his papacy. It is also important to bear in mind that the general mood in 2000 regarding the prospects for peace in the region was much more optimistic than in 2009 following an intifada and several wars later.

Jews tend to be fascinated by the institution of the papacy and yet do not comprehend it. Having one individual with so much authority and institutional power is not something that is part of the Jewish experience. There are subgroups within the Jewish community that surrender to the charisma in certain individuals and see in them figures that are larger-than-life, or even miracle workers. (I'm thinking of some Hassidic groups and certain mystical Jews of Asian or North African backgrounds.) However, the Jewish mainstream is usually skeptical about what might be perceived as a personality cult around an individual religious leader. The issue of how much faith to place in rabbinical pronouncements is hotly debated among Orthodox Jews. There really are no analogues to the hierarchy or magisterium of the Catholic Church.

But—given the above point, perhaps paradoxically—Jews are generally not aware of the diversity that exists within the Church hierarchy. We tend to interpret everything in terms of our own narrow point of reference, without realizing that Church decisions are sometimes made for the sake of unity. For example, the beatification of Pope Pius XII is probably much more a gesture toward the anti–Vatican II forces within the Church—he was, after all, the last pope to serve before the Second Vatican Council—than it is a statement about the Holocaust.

So were there, from a Jewish perspective, any highlights in Pope Benedict's visit? I think there were. During his visit to Jordan, Pope Benedict, like Moses in Deuteronomy, stood on Mount Nebo and viewed the Promised Land; but unlike Moses, he would then actually enter it on the Israeli side. During his talk there, he recalled the "inseparable bond" between Christians and Jews, who share the Hebrew Scriptures. He expressed the desire to "overcome all obstacles to the reconciliation of Christians and Jews in mutual respect and cooperation."

The pope also powerfully acknowledged the deep connection among Jews, the Torah, and the Land of Israel. The anti-Israeli criticism leveled at these remarks and the need for the Vatican spokesman in Jordan to soft-pedal them, saying that the pope was speaking only in a religious vein, showed me how important a statement he had made. When the Royal Jordanian jet landed at Ben-Gurion Airport—a plane of a predominantly Muslim country—it bore the blue-and-white flag of the Jewish State and the yellow flag of the Vatican. Finally, at the welcome ceremony at the airport, the pope condemned unequivocally anti-Semitism and Holocaust denial.

Despite the above, I believe that, as on other occasions as well, the pope received poor guidance from his advisors. Few people paid close attention to the speech at the airport; the eyes of the Jewish world were focused on the visit to Yad Vashem, which was, at best, "lackluster." One might have expected, given his own personal background as a German, and given the flap over Holocaust-denying Bishop Richard Williamson, that the pope would have used the opportunity to say something more significant and to do so in a way that would be more cognizant of special Jewish sensitivities.

In general, Jews lack an understanding of the meaning of pilgrimage for Christians. We are not sufficiently aware of the plight of the local Palestinian Christians. Most Jews also do not realize that since the mutual recognition on the part of the Holy See and the State of Israel in 1993, the two sides have failed to conclude an agreement on a whole range of pressing practical issues. This is no less the "fault" of Israel than it is of the Vatican. An important document called *Dabru Emet* ("Speak [the] Truth") was issued in 2001,[1] calling upon Jews to acknowledge the important changes that have occurred within Christendom vis-à-vis the Jewish people and the State of Israel. Unfortunately, few Jews, outside the limited circles actively engaged in Jewish-Christian dialogue, have ever heard of that document. It is to be hoped that a more recent document, put out by the International Council of Christians and Jews in Berlin 2009, will have wider exposure.[2] This is the first document that calls for parallel processes of historical, catechetical, and liturgical soul-searching on the part of *both* Christians and Jews.

There are a number of outstanding issues within the Catholic-Jewish relationship, some of which were addressed more pointedly in the pope's January 2010 visit to a Rome synagogue than in his pilgrimage to the Holy Land in 2009. One is the status of the Jewish covenantal relationship with God and the validity of our interpretation of Scripture. During Pope Benedict's speech in the synagogue, he quoted from the *Mishnah Avoth* 1:2: "Simon the Just often said: The world is founded on three things, the Torah, worship, and acts of mercy"; in a way he was acknowledging the post-biblical, rabbinic tradition of scriptural interpretation. Ideally, Christians and Jews should be able to learn from and with each other new insights into Scripture, based on their own traditions of interpretation.

Perhaps the thorniest issue—not only for Catholics, but for Christians in general—regards the salvific role of Jesus. If the Jews are in an unbroken covenant with God the Father, why do we need, in order to achieve salvation, to "go through the son" (John 14:6)? This question has arisen perhaps most sharply with regard to the reintroduction of the Tridentine rite for Good Friday and the various versions of the prayers for the Jews.

Finally, there is another question that may ultimately prove to be the most significant for the future of Catholic-Jewish dialogue. It is rarely brought up, if at all. Pope Benedict may very well be the last—or, at least, one of the last—European popes. As John L. Allen has written:

> The pioneers of dialogue on the Catholic side, many
> of whom felt a personal commitment to improving

ties with Judaism because of their memories of the Holocaust, are passing from the scene. Leadership in Catholicism is increasingly coming from Africa, Latin America and Asia, where Judaism is not generally a significant demographic presence. Moreover, Catholics in the global south don't have the same sense of historical responsibility for the Holocaust as Europeans, which they tend to see in terms of Western, rather than Christian, guilt. While these leaders recognize the Biblical roots of the Christian-Jewish relationship, they don't often feel the same biographical commitment to it, nor do they have the same experience of regular interaction and personal friendships with Jews.[3]

One can add to our litany of challenges the rising importance of dialogue with Islam and the identification of many sensitive Catholics with the Palestinians, and against Israel.[4]

I believe that the worldwide Jewish community should invest in locating the future leaders of the Church from these regions, probably at the level of bishops. They should be encouraged to come to Israel for periods of pilgrimage and study, during which they would be exposed to Jewish scholars and dialogue partners. Trilateral dialogue with Christians, Jews, and Muslims could take place as well, under the auspices of organizations like the Inter-religious Coordinating Council in Israel.[5] Some of the infrastructure for this project exists already; there are flourishing institutions for study, at places like Tantur, Ecce Homo, Bat Kol, the Pontifical Biblical Institute in Jerusalem, and so on. The challenge is mainly on an administrative and coordinating level.

I can only hope that Jews involved in interreligious dialogue will realize the importance of such a project, which goes far beyond the question of Pope Pius XII and the Vatican Archives. Here, the real future of our relationship is at stake.

Deborah Weissman, PhD, is a member of the academic staff at the Tantur Ecumenical Institute for Theological Studies, Jerusalem. Born in New York City, she settled in Israel in 1972. Her PhD from the Hebrew University is on the social history of Jewish women's education. She is one of the founding members of Kehillat Yedidya, an Orthodox synagogue in Jerusalem's Bak'a neighborhood, which integrates Halacha (Jewish religious law) with feminism, tolerance, and pluralism. Dr. Weissman is involved with Jewish religious feminism, interfaith dialogue, and the religious peace movement.

1. See www.jcrelations.net/en/?item=1014.
2. See www.iccj.org/en/pdf/BThesen_engl_Kompl.pdf.
3. "This trip may be pope's last chance to see the land of the Bible"—ncronline.org, April 17, 2009. I expressed similar thoughts publicly during a visit to Rome with a delegation of Jewish leaders in October 2008.
4. The whole question of the Israeli-Palestinian conflict and its impact on interreligious dialogue is a crucial one, but it goes far beyond the scope of the present paper.
5. See www.icci.org.il.